Disraeli's
Grand Tour

Disraeli's Grand Tour

Benjamin Disraeli and the Holy Land
1830–31

Robert Blake

///

NEW YORK

OXFORD UNIVERSITY PRESS

1982

© 1982 Robert Blake

First published in Great Britain by
George Weidenfeld and Nicolson Ltd., 1982

First published in the United States
by Oxford University Press, Inc., 1982

ISBN 0-19-520367-4

Library of Congress Catalog Number: 81-48518

Printed in Great Britain

To Victoria

Contents

Acknowledgements   xiii

Introduction   xv

1 GIBRALTAR AND MALTA, MAY–OCTOBER 1830   1

Reasons for Tour – *Alroy* and health – Disraeli's nervous
illness – Debts and *Vivian Grey* – Raises money by writing
The Young Duke – Improved health – Companion for the
Tour – Meredith, a sedate young man – They sail from
Falmouth – Nature of his Home Letters – Disraeli's family
– Arrival in Gibraltar – Hospitality of Governor – Lawless
state of Spain – Disraeli lectures a bore on canes – Visit to
Cadiz, Seville and Granada – Disraeli mistaken for a Moor
– Malta – James Clay – His yacht and 'Tita' – A revealing
letter – Clay's sexual prowess and dissipated character –
Disraeli's affected conduct in the Fives Court – His foppish
dress – They sail to Corfu in Clay's yacht

2 CORFU AND ALBANIA, OCTOBER 1830   27

Condition of Corfu – Rebellion in Albania – Disraeli's plan
to join Grand Vizier's forces – His pro-Turk sentiments –
His contempt for Greeks – Plan frustrated by Turkish
victory – Bears a message from Governor of Corfu – Greek
war of independence – Atrocious conduct on each side –
The trio sail to Prevesa and Salora – Overland journey to

Yanina – They get drunk with a Bey on the way – Desolate
state of Yanina – Disraeli fascinated by oriental glamour –
Audience with Grand Vizier – His debauched son – Return
to Prevesa

3 GREECE AND CONSTANTINOPLE,
OCTOBER 1830–JANUARY 1831   43

Greek situation in 1830 – Voyage along coast of Hellas and
Morea – Excursions from Nauplion – Crown of Greece –
Athens and the Acropolis – Wild boar and honey – Vermin
– Constantinople – Nature of Turkish rule – Its sloth,
cruelty and incompetence – Its capacity for survival –
Affability of British Ambassador – Open invitation to
dinner and picnic – Meredith goes to Bithynian mountains
– Disraeli studies *Galignani's Messenger* – Description of
Constantinople and the Sultan – Perfect climate – Lasting
effect of his Turkish experience

4 THE HOLY CITY, JANUARY–MARCH 1831   59

Disraeli and Clay sail to Smyrna – Meet up with Meredith
– He separates again – Cyprus – Jaffa – The orientalized
Venetian Damiani – An excellent dinner – Journey to
Jerusalem – Perils of travel – Disraeli's impression of the
city from Mount of Olives – Condition of Jerusalem at this
time – St Salvador – Clarke's description – Holy Sepulchre
– Mosque of Omar – Politico-religious situation in
Palestine – Moslem, Jewish and Christian quarters in
Jerusalem – Disraeli not a 'Jew' – Christian feuds – *Tancred*
– Mehemet Ali's conquest of Syria – the Anglican Bishopric
of Jerusalem

5 THE LAND OF PRIESTCRAFT AND PYRAMIDS,
MARCH–OCTOBER 1831   79

Disraeli and Clay in Alexandria – Meredith rejoins them –
Egyptian recent history – Napoleon's expedition –
Triumph of Mehemet Ali – Political news from England –
Clay and 'Tita' ill – Disraeli's excellent health – Lives *à la
Turque* – Loses his best servant – News from home – Death
of 'Max' and Isaac D'Israeli's epitaph – Journey from
Alexandria to Cairo – Three week voyage up Nile – Terrors
of a 'Simoom' – Splendours of Thebes – Audiences with
Mehemet Ali – Moral drawn by Disraeli – Acquaintance-
ship with Botta – His 'curious' letters – Meredith dies of
smallpox – Disraeli returns to England – The Henry Stanley
imbroglio – Disraeli's innocence – 'A course of mercury'

6 THE AFTERMATH   103

Effects on Disraeli – Improvement in health – Importance
of Jerusalem – His interest in the 'Court Jews' of the Near
East – Effect on his novels – Passages in *Contarini Fleming* –
Rise of Iskander – Significance of *Alroy* – Disraeli's 'ideal
ambition'–*Alroy*, symbol of an alien rising to the top ? –
Tancred – Description of the story – Disraeli's idea of the
Church–Tancred's determination to see the Holy Land –
Horror of his family – Efforts to stop him – His experiences
in Palestine – A bathetic ending – Disraeli's ambiguous
status – Position of Jews in England – Not persecuted but
not liked – Disraeli creates myth of a superior race –
Compensation for coming from the fringe – A problem of
identity – Disraeli and Zionism – A curious conversation
with Lord Stanley in 1851 – A dream ? – 'The haunting
voice of the prophets'

Index   135

Illustrations

Between pages 46 and 47

Isaac D'Israeli *(Mansell Collection)*
Sarah D'Israeli *(National Trust, Hughenden Manor)*
Line drawing of the young Disraeli *(Mary Evans Picture Library)*
James Clay *(National Trust, Hughenden Manor)*
Byron in Albanian dress *(National Portrait Gallery)*
Tita *(National Trust, Hughenden Manor)*
Corfu *(Mary Evans Picture Library)*
Yanina (Weidenfeld and Nicolson Archives)

Between pages 78 and 79

The Turks capturing Missolonghi in 1826 *(Mary Evans Picture Library)*
Athens and the Acropolis (Weidenfeld and Nicolson Archives)
Constantinople from the Bosphorus *(Mansell Collection)*
Sultan Mahmoud II (Weidenfeld and Nicolson Archives)
The Great Bazaar at Constantinople *(Mary Evans Picture Library)*
The Mosque of Sultan Ahmet, Constantinople *(Mary Evans Picture Library)*
View of Jerusalem *(Mansell Collection)*

Between pages 110 and 111

The Mosque of Omar, in the Muslim quarter of Jerusalem *(Mansell Collection)*
The Pool of Hezekiah, Jerusalem *(Mansell Collection)*
The Church of the Holy Sepulchre, Jerusalem *(Mansell Collection)*

Illustrations

Mehemet Ali *(Mary Evans Picture Library)*
Street scene in Cairo *(Mansell Collection)*
Paul Emile Botta *(Louvre, Paris)*
Edward Stanley, 14th Earl of Derby *(Mary Evans Picture Library)*
The Great Temple of Abu Simbel, Nubia *(Mansell Collection)*

Acknowledgements

I would like to thank the Editorial Board of the Disraeli Project at Queen's University, Kingston, Ontario for making available to me their transcript of Disraeli's Home Letters, thus saving me the trouble of copying out extracts from the Disraeli Papers in the Bodleian Library. The published version of these, edited by Ralph Disraeli (1885), is full of errors. I have retained most of Disraeli's rather eccentric spelling but I have made some changes in his equally eccentric punctuation.

I would also like to thank Mr Benjamin Buchan of Weidenfeld and Nicolson for copyediting the text and for providing the illustrations, and my secretary, Miss Angela Payne, for typing and re-typing the MS.

Introduction

In October 1966, after some eight years' work, I published a long single-volume biography of Disraeli. At that time my only two visits to what used to be called Palestine had been short and fleeting. I was briefly stationed as a subaltern in a gunner regiment near Acre in the autumn of 1941. There was a chance of leave to see Jerusalem but we had to draw lots for the privilege, and I was unlucky. A few days later the regiment set out clanking along the dreary route which followed the pipe-line from Haifa to Iraq. Although we returned a couple of months later, we were then merely in transit for Cairo and the Western Desert, and there was no chance of sight-seeing.

It was not till the spring of 1979 that I saw Jerusalem. I spent six weeks there as a guest in Mishkenot Sha'anannim, commanding a splendid view of the Old City from the south. The experience was a memorable one. Jerusalem must be one of the most fascinating cities in the world. In retrospect I think that I ought to have gone earlier, sometime during the years which I spent in writing my biography. There was no particular reason why I should not have done so, but, as Dr Johnson observes of Alexander Pope's slowness in producing his translation of the *Iliad*, 'Indolence, interruption, business and pleasure, all take their turns of retardation; and every long work is lengthened by a thousand causes that can, and ten thousand that cannot be recounted.' Eight years was quite long enough, and I wanted to finish.

My visit to Jerusalem, however, made me read again many works by and about Disraeli, including my own and his novels, and above all his letters describing his tour of the Near East. It also made me think again about the effect upon him of his stay in Jerusalem. However briefly he describes it in his letters, a re-reading of some of his (admittedly least readable) novels suggests that the experience really was important. I felt that I had not perhaps done it full justice in my biography. I had forgotten, too, what fun his letters are to read. There is zest, vigour, love of life, conceit, wit, impertinence, romanticism. He is one of the best letter-writers since Byron. Therefore when Lord Weidenfeld suggested a short book on the subject I was happy to accept.

This is not a book which contains significant new material. The letters from which I quote have for the most part (though not all) appeared somewhere or other (albeit in garbled form), scattered over various publications. I am, however, encouraged by the late Sir Lewis Namier's dictum that 'most secrets are in print if you know where to look for them'. The book's justification is an attempt to re-examine a crucial period in the strange career of one of the strangest Prime Ministers in English history. But I am well aware of the observations of Professor John Vincent in the best short essay on Disraeli in recent times1 : 'We shall never know Disraeli well. His intimates did not Boswellise him. His inner thoughts on the Jewish people, for instance, could hardly hope for a sympathetic hearing. The real degree of his enthusiasm or distaste for the English aristocracy . . . is unknowable.' This is true, and there must be a more than normal degree of guesswork in any book that purports to explain what his *bête noire*, Bentham, would have called his 'springs of action'. Nevertheless, with all allowance made for the speculative nature of any attempt to delve into Disraeli's psychology, I do believe that his tour of the Near East, and in particular his week in Jerusalem, had a profound influence upon him, and that an effort to analyse it is worth making.

The Queen's College, Oxford   *Robert Blake*
June 1981

1 *The Prime Ministers*, ed. H. van Thal, vol. 2 (1975), p. 106.

Disraeli's
Grand Tour

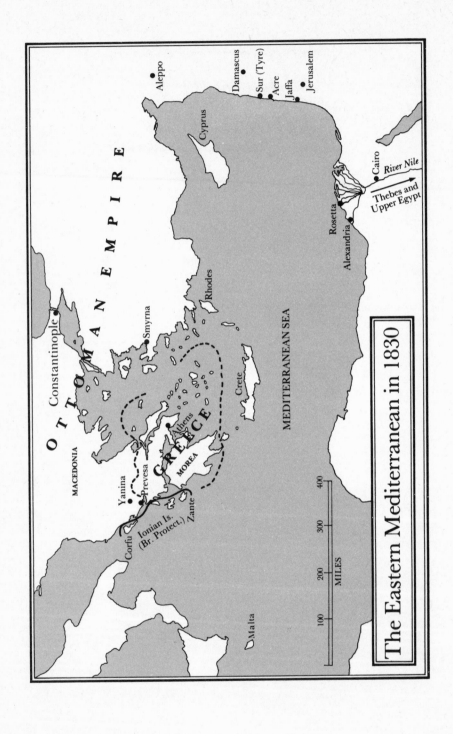

The Eastern Mediterranean in 1830

Chapter 1
Gibraltar and Malta
May–October 1830

I

Benjamin Disraeli's tour of the Mediterranean and the Near East in 1830–31 was one of the formative experiences of his career. He was twenty-five when he set out, and the impressions that it made on him were life-lasting. They conditioned his attitude towards some of the most important political problems which faced him in his later years – especially the Eastern Question ; they also coloured many of his novels – *Contarini Fleming*, *Alroy*, *Tancred*, *Lothair* and others. One of his reasons for the tour was to secure 'copy' for *Alroy*, which he claims that he had already begun and which is based on a legendary Jewish hero of the twelfth century, alleged to have sought to win back the independence of Israel from the decaying Caliphate. It is a very bad novel – indeed one of his worst, but it is highly revealing about Disraeli.

His other and stronger reason was to restore himself to health. From early 1827 till the end of 1829 he had suffered from a mysterious psychosomatic malady. Its exact nature is unknown. The symptoms were lethargy, exhaustion, depression and inertia. His father, Isaac, had in his youth endured something very similar. It would probably be called in modern times a 'nervous breakdown' or 'mental illness'. No one can be sure what causes such maladies but in Benjamin's case it does not seem fanciful to link it with his feverish and turbulent existence for the two years from November 1824 when, as he puts it in *Vivian Grey*, 'the hour of adventure had arrived'. He began by disastrous speculation on the margin in South American mining shares, together with two young friends in the City. He was at this time an articled clerk with a firm of London solicitors. The trio bought at the top and sold at the bottom with unerring accuracy, which resulted in an adverse balance of £7,000 by June 1826. Disraeli's liability was the origin of a load of debt which, multiplied many times over by reckless improvidence, hung round his neck long into middle age. To arrest the decline of the companies in which he had speculated, he published on commission with John Murray, his father's old friend, a series of pamphlets early in 1825 extolling what he must have known to be very dubious concerns – a unique literary debut for a future statesman, and quite ineffectual, for the fall continued.

Still hoping for a turn of the tide, Disraeli now involved himself in another disastrous enterprise – a partnership with Murray and one J.D.Powles, a prominent merchant in South American trade, to set up a new paper as a rival to *The Times*. He signed a document on 3 August 1825 guaranteeing a quarter of the capital and twice rushed up to Scotland to secure Sir Walter Scott's son-in-law, J.G.Lockhart, as 'Director-General'. He failed to get his acceptance and succeeded only in arousing his life-long enmity and Murray's suspicions. He busied himself with recruiting correspondents, conferring with lawyers and architects, negotiating with printers. This whirl of frenetic activity ended abruptly just before Christmas – probably because the great stock-market crash of December finally obliterated whatever chance there was of him supplying his share of the capital. The *Representative*, as it was called, appeared on 25 January 1826, by which time Disraeli was out of the affair altogether. It was a complete flop from the start, costing Murray £26,000 before he cut his losses and closed it down six months later.

Undeterred by these disasters Disraeli resolved to recoup some of his losses by writing. Part 1 of *Vivian Grey* appeared anonymously on 22 April under the imprint of Henry Colburn, a slightly shady publisher who gave him £200 and puffed the author as a 'man of fashion'. It is an amusing, affected, brash, impudent 'silver fork' novel, thinly disguising the story of the *Representative* transposed from journalism into politics and high society. John Murray, who is caricatured as the Marquis of Carabas, a pompous tipsy nincompoop, was understandably furious and the episode led to a lasting breach not only with Benjamin but the whole D'Israeli family. The authorship soon leaked out and the reviewers, discovering that the writer, far from being a man of fashion, was a solicitor's articled clerk of twenty-one, cut the book to pieces. Disraeli looked back with no pleasure on these episodes of his early life and did all he could to erase the record.

At the beginning of August 1826, exhausted by his efforts, he went on a three-month tour of Switzerland and Italy. His companions were a dull and rather prosy London solicitor, Benjamin Austen, from whom he was later to borrow money, and his wife Sara, who, one can guess, was half in love with Disraeli and who had acted as amanuensis, agent, go-between and proof corrector for *Vivian Grey*. Disraeli never forgot one experience – being rowed by Byron's boatman, Maurice, on the Lake of Geneva on a warm night amidst a sensational display of lightning without a drop of rain. The holiday brought no relief. That winter, desperate for money, he wrote Part II of *Vivian Grey*, which, unlike Part I, was inoffensive and dull. It appeared on 23 February 1827 and produced a welcome £500, but he then collapsed into a state of mental and physical exhaustion. For nearly three years his life was a blank, though he managed to produce a rather slight novel, *The Voyage of Captain Popanilla*, in 1828.

Whatever the nature and cause of his malady, it was real enough. His family were seriously worried. There are hints that his mind was at one time deranged and his life at another despaired of. Isaac D'Israeli's home was still in London but he took houses by the sea or in the country in order to give his eldest son the 'change of air' prescribed by doctors who could think of nothing else. In 1829 Isaac moved permanently into the country, taking a long lease of Bradenham House, which still stands, a beautiful red-brick Queen Anne building, two or three miles north of West Wycombe in Buckinghamshire. Various doctors were tried, the least unsuccessful being a Dr Buckley Bolton, with whose wife, Clara, Disraeli had an affair, possibly beginning in 1829 or early 1830 at Bradenham and apparently in full swing in 1832 when he was making his way in London society after his return from the East. Whether for this or some other reason Disraeli's health improved enough for him to set about his arrangements for his Grand Tour. His father disapproved and was not willing to produce the money. So he resolved to drop *Alroy* and raise the funds by an avowed pot-boiler. He wrote to Austen on 8 December 1829 :

> The fact is that I am 'spell bound within the clustering Cyclades' [a quotation from Byron, referring to the archipelago centred on the Greek island of Syros] and go I must, tho' I fear I must hack for it. A literary prostitute I have never yet been, tho' born in an age of general prostitution and tho' I have more than once been subject to temptations which might have been the ruination of a less virtuous young man. My mind, however, is still a virgin, but the mystical flower, I fear, must soon be plucked – Colburn, I suppose will be the bawd. Tempting Mother Colburn.

Colburn was willing. Disraeli rapidly completed *The Young Duke* by March 1830, observing to William Meredith, his friend and his sister's fiancé : 'I am confident of its success and that it will complete the corruption of the public taste.' Colburn paid £500 in post-dated bills, against which Austen gave Disraeli a letter of credit for the same sum to be drawn upon at Malta, Smyrna and Constantinople. *The Young Duke* was not published till 1831 and is as affected and artificial as *Vivian Grey* ('What does Ben know of dukes ?' his father asked), but it served its purpose and he could go at last.

Disraeli at once bounced up from his state of depression into one of euphoria. He hastened to London with the manuscript of the novel at the end of March, having taken precautions against arrest for debt – one of his constant bugbears, indeed an additional reason for getting out of the country – and resolved to cut a dash. He was twenty-five and must have seemed one of the most foppish, insufferable, conceited young men that ever walked. William Meredith noted in his diary : 'B.D. to dine with me. He came up Regent Street when it was crowded, in his blue surtout, a pair of military light blue trousers, black stockings with red stripes and shoes [most people wore boots in those days]. "The people," he said, "quite made way for me as I passed. It was like the opening of the Red Sea which I now perfectly believe from experience." I should think so !' On the same visit, dining for the first time with Bulwer-Lytton, whom he had contacted through his father, one of Bulwer's heroes, he wore, so Bulwer's brother Henry wrote, 'green velvet trousers, a canary coloured waistcoat, low shoes, silver buckles, lace at his wrists and his hair in ringlets'. Alexander Cockburn, a future Lord Chief Justice, and Charles Villiers, a future cabinet minister, both celebrated for their wit, made up the company. But the writer added : 'If on leaving the table we had been severally taken aside and asked which was the cleverest of the party we should have been obliged to say "the man in the green velvet trousers".'

Disraeli's companion on his tour was William Meredith. He was a grave, sedate, serious-minded and virtuous young man who had known the D'Israeli family all his life. He was utterly unlike Benjamin. His letters and journal dealing with some of the same experiences show no trace of Disraeli's wit, gaiety and sparkle, though they may well be more accurate. He had been engaged to Disraeli's sister for some time, but, although he had money, marriage was delayed because there was the prospect of more ; he was the heir to a rich uncle who disapproved of the match – probably because of the Jewish connexion. However, William managed to square things with the uncle just before he left England. The wedding was to take place on their return. The tour would be William's last 'fling' – not that he was addicted to 'flings' – as a bachelor. One can guess that the D'Israeli family was relieved to see their most wayward and eccentric member accompanied by a friend of such respectability.

On Friday, 28 May the two young men set out on the first leg of their journey – from London to Falmouth by sea. The weather was very rough. But Disraeli, having arrived at four in the morning, wrote to his sister on 1 June from the Royal Hotel : 'I was not only not sick, but did not feel a qualm. Meredith quite well but he cannot match me as a sailor. So far, so good, but for the rest the steam packet is a beastly conveyance, and the total absence of all comfort, decency and refinement is trying.' They were detained in Falmouth ('one of the most charming places I ever saw') for a week, but it gave them time to 'buy bedding for the Mediterranean packets – a bore'. The plan had been to go straight to Malta but, for whatever reason, they found it convenient to stop at Gibraltar first. Disraeli's next letter is from the Rock.

His adventures on his travels are mainly known from his letters. Most are to the family and are usually called the *Home Letters*, very badly edited by his brother Ralph, but he wrote to others, among them Sara and Benjamin Austen – to the latter usually with some money problem embedded – and to Bulwer-Lytton, who was every bit as dandified, vain and egotistical as he was. Nevertheless they had struck up a close friendship, though it was not to survive their youth and marriages. Most of the *Home Letters* were written to Isaac, some to his sister Sarah, and one each to his mother and to Ralph. They were clearly intended to be read to the family as descriptions of scenes, episodes and people, and to be recovered on his return for incorporation almost verbatim in his next novel.

Isaac D'Israeli was sixty-four when Benjamin left England. He encouraged and appreciated, though with occasional warnings, his son's talents. In return Disraeli thought most highly of his father, putting him, characteristically, as one of the only three people from whose conversation he had profited. Isaac was well known in the literary world. He had written poetry, history and novels. His poem 'To Laura' was included in Walter Scott's *English Minstrelsy* and his historical works were praised by Southey. But his chief fame was as a compiler of literary episodes and anecdotes. His highly idiosyncratic *Curiosities of Literature* went into edition after edition long beyond his death. Byron, a great admirer, wrote of him, 'He is the Bayle of literary speculation, who puts together more amusing information than anyone.' Isaac was a man of some means, inherited partly from a doting grandmother whose will made him financially independent at twenty-four, and partly from his father, Benjamin the elder, straw-hat merchant and stockbroker, who left £35,000 in 1816. The family came from Italy, not Spain as the younger Benjamin romantically imagined – Spanish Jewry having a more dramatic and intriguing history. They belonged to the Sephardic branch of the Jewish faith, but Isaac, despite writing a book called *The Genius of Judaism*, took no great interest in the religion of his forebears. He was currently engaged on a five-volume work about Charles I, which in 1832 brought him an honorary Doctorship of Civil Law from the University of Oxford, ever loyal to the glorious memory of Charles the Martyr.

Although his son liked to portray him as a genial good-humoured recluse and a scholarly denizen of libraries, Isaac was by no means always an urbane figure. He was frequently involved in furious literary and historical disputes where he gave as good as he got in terms of vituperation and abuse. Attacked by a critic he replied unconvincingly that he did not mind corrections, but 'it is loathsome to pick them out of a filthy platter heaved at us by the hoof of a literary Yahoo'. Another critic he described as 'a Mole ; a diminutive and grubbing animal which fears the light and exhausts its feeble and industrious malice by injuring the grounds of everyone'. The exchange of pamphlets between him and the antiquarian, Bolton Corney, who attacked *Curiosities of Literature*, reminds one of nothing so much as a greatly expanded version of the sort of disputation so often to be read in the columns of the modern *Times Literary Supplement*.

Disraeli's mother Maria (née Basevi), also of Sephardic Italian origin, is a more shadowy figure. She was a busy wife, mother and manager of household affairs, servants, cooks, menus etc. She did not give her eldest son the admiration, let alone the adoration, which he craved. In the row with John Murray about the *Representative* she wrote to that great publisher describing Benjamin as being : 'tho' a clever boy . . . no "prodigy".' Disraeli may well never have seen the letter but he would have sensed the attitude long before. Such muted praise was not good enough for him. His silence about her in his letters, papers and publications speaks for itself.

He had an elder sister and two younger brothers. Sarah, two years older, who was born in 1802 and died in 1864, was, apart from Isaac, the only member of the family who had something of Disraeli's mental ability and power of expression. She was fond of her brother and believed in his future. Later, after the tragic death of Meredith (see Chapter 5) and having abandoned all idea of marriage, she became his acolyte and devotee, but at this time she was not uncritical. 'You have been too gay and too dissipated among your Maltese heroes,' she wrote to him on 4 December 1830, having heard that he was leaving the island for Corfu, 'and I flatter myself that a little hard biscuit and salt water, good naval discipline, have superseded the vinous propensities of your friends.' However, she ended, 'Goodbye, dearest Ben. May God bless and preserve you for us and for the world.'

Disraeli's brothers had little or no share of his temperament and talent. Both, unlike Benjamin (who attended in succession two long-forgotten minor private schools), were sent to Winchester. The elder of the two, Ralph, who was born in 1809, lived till he was nearly ninety. He was the only brother to beget legitimate children. At the time when the present author began his biography of Disraeli in 1958, a Miss Disraeli, Ralph's daughter, was still alive. Ralph's son, Coningsby, was Disraeli's heir and inherited Hughenden on his uncle's death in 1881. Ralph became a clerk in Chancery and later Clerk Assistant in the House of Lords, ending up as Deputy Clerk of Parliaments. He was touchy and slightly jealous. The younger brother, James, known as 'Jem', was born in 1813 and died in 1868. He was something of a nuisance to his distinguished eldest brother, having what the latter called 'low connexions'. Eventually Benjamin managed to place him as Commissioner of Excise. There is a rather pathetic letter among Disraeli's papers from a woman who was, or believed herself to be, an illegitimate daughter of James.

2

The two travellers arrived at Gibraltar on HMS *Messenger* in mid-June. Disraeli's first two letters from abroad are to his father, both sent on 1 July. They had an introduction to a Dr Alexander Broad-foot, Assistant Inspector of Health in Gibraltar. He was most helpful and friendly and presented them to the Lieutenant Governor, General Sir George Don, 'a very fine old gentleman of the Windsor Terrace School, courtly almost regal in his manner', as Disraeli put it in one of his letters to Isaac. He was a rich man and spent much from his personal resources on beautifying the place.

> His palace, the Government House, is an old convent and one of the most delightful residences I know, with a garden under the superintendence of Lady Don full of rare exotics with a beautiful Terrace over the sea, a *berceau* of vines, and other delicacies which would delight you. Besides this Sir Geo. has a delightful Pavillion modestly called the Cottage at the extreme point of the Rock, and a villa at San Roque in Spain about 10 miles off. Thus by a constant change of residence, he counteracts the monotony of his situation. He possesses a large private fortune, all of which he here disburses, and has ornamented Gibraltar, as a lover does his mistress.

Sir George Don had, according to Disraeli, even gone so far as to spend his money on improving the almost non-existent communications in southern Spain. 'Gibraltar is a limited theatre for His

Excellency, and he has civilized Spain for twenty miles round, by making roads, building bridges, and reforming *posadas* [i.e. inns]'. His hospitality to Disraeli and Meredith was frequent and lavish. He made them partake of his favourite beverage, 'half champagne and half lemonade' – a slight variation on what would now be called 'Buck's Fizz'.

'This rock,' wrote Disraeli, 'is a wonderful place with a population infinitely diversified – Moors with costumes radiant as a rainbow . . . Jews with gaberdines and scull caps, Genoese, Highlanders and Spaniards, whose dress is as picturesque as the sons of Ivor.' The two libraries at Gibraltar not only contained all Isaac's works but 'another book said to be written by a member of our family, and which is looked upon at Gibraltar as one of the masterpieces of the 19th century. You may feel their intellectual pulse from this.' The book of course is *Vivian Grey*, of which Disraeli was far from proud. He apologised at first and 'talked of youthful blunders' but when he found to his surprise that the novel really was admired he quickly went into reverse. 'Fearing they were stupid enough to adopt my last opinion I shifted my position just in time, looked very grand and passed myself off for a child of the sun like the Spaniards in Peru.'

At Sir George Don's suggestion Disraeli and Meredith went on a week's excursion to Spain in the Sierra da Ronda, 'a savage mountain district abounding in the most beautiful scenery and bugs'. It was, Disraeli alleged, 'a land entirely of robbers and smugglers. They commit no personal violence but lay you on the ground and clean out your pockets. If you have less than sixteen dollars they shoot you; that is the tariff, and is a loss worth risking.' Spain at this time was governed by a ferocious, Bourbon, clerical reactionary (in the literal sense). Ferdinand vii had ruled since 1815 with complete autocracy except for a brief 'liberal' interlude in 1821–3. The country was sunk in poverty and lawlessness. The royal régime was good at hanging liberals but bad at preventing brigandage. Three years later the King's death, which led to the Carlist wars, reduced the country to an even worse state than at the time of Disraeli's visit. He does not say much in his letters about politics, merely noting that the semi-savageness of the inhabitants made each district retain its customs and dress 'with barbarous jealousy', also that 'a weak government resolves society into its original elements and robbery becomes more honourable than war, inasmuch as the robber is paid and the soldier is in arrear' – not a very profound thought even for a young man of twenty-five.

Few Englishmen visited southern Spain in those days. There were scarcely any roads. The traveller went on horseback by what Disraeli describes as a 'course which can only be compared to the steep bed of an exhausted cataract'. The inns or *posadas* were like 'a caravanserai', a mere shelter for the night. It was necessary to cater for oneself for provisions and to cook them, or arrange for them to be cooked by others. Luckily Disraeli and his friend had acquired an excellent factotum.

Above all we have Brunet. What a man ! Born in Italy of French parents, he has visited as the Captain of a Privateer all the countries of the Mediterranean – Egypt, Turkey, Syria. Early in life as valet to Lord Hood he was in England and has even been at Guinea. After fourteen years cruising, he was taken by the Algerines, and was in various parts of Barbary for five or six years. At last he obtains his liberty and settles at Gibraltar, where he becomes Cacador to the Governor, for he is, among his universal accomplishments, a celebrated shot. He can speak all languages but English of which he makes a sad affair – even Latin, and he hints at a little Greek. He is fifty, but light as a butterfly, and gay as a bird; in person not unlike English at Lyme, if you can imagine so insipid a character with a vivacity that never flags, and a tongue that never rests. Brunet did everything, remedied every inconvenience, and found an expedient for every difficulty. Never did I live so well as among these wild mountains of Andalusia, so exquisite is his cookery. Seriously he is an artist of the first magnitude, and used to amuse himself by giving us some very exquisite dish among these barbarians, for he affects a great contempt of the Spaniards, and an equal admiration of the Moors. Whenever we complained, he shrugged his shoulders with a look of ineffable contempt exclaiming '*Nous ne sommes pas in Barbarie* !' Recalling our associations with that word and country, it was superbly ludicrous.

Fortunately Disraeli and Meredith were not robbed, though their first experience on returning to Griffiths Hotel in Gibraltar was to meet two Englishmen who had been stripped of all their possessions at a village which Disraeli had visited only a day or so earlier.

Disraeli, back in Gibraltar, played up to his part as a dandy.

I maintain my reputation of being a great judge of costume to the admiration and envy of many subalterns. I have also the fame of being the first who ever passed the Straits with two canes, a morning and an evening cane. I change my cane as the gun fires, and hope to carry them both on to Cairo. It is wonderful the effect these magical wands produce.

However there were snags even in this carefree life. For example, there was the Advocate General, 'a bore and vulgar . . .'

Consequently I gave him a lecture on canes which made him stare, and he has avoided me ever since. The truth is he wished to saddle his brother upon me as a compagnon de voyage, whom I discovered in the course of half an hour to be both deaf, dumb, and blind, yet more endurable than the noisy, obtrusive, jargonic judge, who is a true lawyer, ever illustrating the obvious, explaining the evident, and expatiating on the commonplace.

The original plan of the two travellers had been to sail as early as possible for Malta, but the delights of southern Spain made them linger in that area for two months. They first went to Cadiz on 14 July : ' "Fair Florence" is a very dingy affair compared with it. The white houses and green jalousies sparkle in the sun. Figaro is in every street, and Rosina in every balcony.' On 26 July they were in Seville.

'The place is fearfully hot,' he wrote to Isaac, 'hot enough even for me, but the heat agrees with my constitution and even my head is better.' But Disraeli did not wish to give his father the impression that his health had been restored. 'The improvement is, however, very slight, and it will be at best a long affair. If I could get on as well as I have done this fortnight though, I should have hope. My general health is most remarkable.' The passage makes one again wonder about the nature of Disraeli's illness. Did he suffer from attacks of migraine? What did he really mean by the 'palpitations of the heart' to which he often refers ? It is not at all clear.

On 1 August Disraeli was writing to his mother from Granada (which he spelt like the West Indian island) a long letter about life in Spain. Never one to waste a good thing, he used most of it verbatim in *Contarini Fleming*, Part V, Chapters 6 and 7. He describes the ladies – 'You know that I am rather an admirer of the blonde . . . But las Espagnolos are nevertheless very interesting personages' – luxuriant hair, their black *mantillas*, and their tortoiseshell combs. He discusses the fruit and wishes that his father was there too to enjoy 'a medley of grape and melon, gourd and prickly pear'. He is not enthusiastic in general about Spanish cooking – too much garlic and bad oil, but the soups are good and '*the most agreeable dish* in the world is an Olio'. This apparently consisted of a mixture of 'bouilli' beef, pork sausage and black pudding with vegetables, mostly French beans, slices of melon and pears. 'Mix them in your plate together and drown them in a tomata [sic] sauce. There is no garlic and no grease of any kind. I have eaten this every day.' He went on to give a recipe for tomato sauce 'Take four pounds of Tomatas, fry them very small ; add four eggs, yolk and all. Mix well. They should be served very dry . . . I need not tell the mistress of so experienced a cuisine as you to add a small quantity of onion in frying the tomatas.'

But the same letter contains despondent remarks about his head. 'The moment I attempt to meditate . . . or in any way call the greater powers of intellect into operation, that moment I feel a lost man. The palpitation in my heart and head increases in violence, an indescribable feeling of idiocy comes over me, and for hours I am plunged in a

15

state of the darkest despair.' If he is not cured by the end of a year's travel, 'I resign myself to my fate'. If he was a Catholic, he 'would then enter a Convent, but as I am a member of a family to which I am devotedly attached and a good Protestant I shall return to them and to my country, but to a solitary room which I never leave. I see no one and speak with no one. I am serious. Prepare yourself for this . . .' It does not sound a particularly cheerful prospect for the D'Israeli family, but one does not know how seriously they took Benjamin's intermittent lugubrious vaticinations – probably not very. He admitted that there was improvement. 'You know how much better I am on a sunny day in England – well I have had two months of sunny days infinitely warmer.' He finished the letter with a sparkling account of the evening promenade, the sea breeze, the warm moonlight. 'The last guitar dies away and the Cathedral clock breaks up your reverie. You too seek your couch, and amid a sweet flow of loveliness and light, and music and fresh air, thus dies a day in Spain.'

Disraeli and Meredith visited the famous places. At Seville they went to the Alcazar, at Cordova they saw the shrine of a Moorish saint and observed 'the blue mosaic and the golden honeycombed roof as vivid and as brilliant as when the saint was first worshipped.' In Granada they repaired to the Alhambra. Meredith noted that the old lady who showed them over this splendid edifice was quite convinced that 'Benjamin D. was a Moor, many of whom come to visit this palace, which, they say, will be theirs yet again. His southern aspect, the style in which he paced the gorgeous apartments and sat himself in the seat of the Abencerrages quite deceived her.'

On 8 August they were back in Gibraltar. Disraeli wrote next day to his sister :

With regard to my plans we are certainly off next packet, perhaps on Saturday [August 14]. No further can I aver. What use are plans? Did I dream 6 months ago of Andalusia where I have spent some of the most agreeable hours of my existence. Such a trip ! Such universal novelty and such unrivalled luck in all things.

And at the end of a long letter, he wrote :

Oh! Wonderful Spain! Think of this romantic land covered with Moorish ruins and full of Murillo! Ah! that I could describe to you the wonders of the painted temples of Seville, ah! that I could wander with you amid the fantastic and imaginative halls of delicate Alhambra ! Why, why, cannot I convey to you more perfectly all that I see and feel! I thought that enthusiasm was dead within me, and nothing could be new. I have hit perhaps upon the only country which could have upset my theory, a country of which I have read little, and thought nothing, a country of which indeed nothing has been written and which few visit. I dare to say that I am better. This last fortnight I have made regular progress, or rather felt perhaps the progress which I had already made. It is all the Sun. Do not think that it is society or change of scene. This, however occasionally agreable, is too much for me, and ever throws me back. It is when I am quite alone, and quite still, that I feel the difference of my system, that I miss old aches, and am conscious of the increased activity and vitality and expansion of my blood.

Disraeli and Meredith took the packet from Gibraltar at last and landed in Malta on 19 August. They were lodged for a week in quarantine in the Lazaretto, 'imprisoned in a vast and solitary building, and shunned by my fellow men,' as Disraeli wrote. Malta, as the gateway to Europe from North Africa and the Near East, had strict rules about infectious diseases, and cholera was at this time on the rise. 'Lazaretto' originally meant a hospital for those suffering from leprosy and other contagious diseases. The word later came to signify an institution to detain people who were quarantined. There are many plaintive references in letters and journals of contemporary travellers to the tedium of this experience.

The journey in the steam packet had been anything but agreeable, 'a very rough and disagreeable voyage, the wind the devil of a Levanter i.e. from the east and sometimes Scirocc, full in our teeth half the time and not going even with steam more than four knots an hour . . . The sky was covered with clouds nearly the whole time.' The only pleasant interlude was to put in at Algiers, recently seized by Bourbon France but appropriately flying the Tricolour after the bloodless revolution in Paris which had installed Louis Philippe a week or so earlier on 28 July. A month before there had been a peaceful change of monarch in England: William IV had succeeded his brother. At that time the death of the King entailed a general election. Austen, writing to Disraeli, said that he was sorry Disraeli would miss a chance to take part in the campaign, 'It would be a famous opening & lots to say.' The travellers were out of quarantine by 27 August and 'quartered in a capital hotel – Beverley's', which contrasted with Gibraltar 'where our quarters were horrid'.

3

At this moment they met an old acquaintance, James Clay, who was to be with Disraeli for the rest of the tour. He was only a year younger than Disraeli but he had overlapped at Winchester with Ralph, who came to know him well then or later. He went up to Balliol and was an Oxford contemporary of Meredith, who was at Brasenose and who disapproved of him. He was a wealthy young man, and he was very good-looking, with the complexion of a ripe peach if his portrait at Hughenden can be relied upon. His father and grandfather, who stemmed from Derbyshire, were rich City merchants and shipowners in London. His uncle, Sir William Clay, was Liberal MP for Tower Hamlets 1832–57 and a member of Melbourne's government 1839–41. For his services he was given a baronetcy which is still extant.

Clay had chartered a fifty-five-ton yacht in which he offered to convey Disraeli and Meredith eastwards. He had another notable asset in Byron's former gondolier and manservant, Giovanni Battista Falcieri, who had been at his master's deathbed in Missolonghi six years before. Known sometimes as 'Giovanni', sometimes as 'Tita', he was an engaging figure. Shelley decribed him as 'a fine fellow with a prodigious black beard who has stabbed two or three people and is the most good-natured fellow I ever saw'. Disraeli in his usual hyperbolic style wrote : 'His moustachios touch the earth. Withall mild as a lamb tho' daggers always about his person.'

Clay was a vigorous games player, energetic and athletic. The activity, however, in which he really excelled was sexual intercourse. He was a strenuous womaniser from early youth. Sixteen months later, when the tour had ended and the trio were dispersed or dead, he wrote a letter to Disraeli on 21 December 1831, Disraeli's birthday. It was from the Lazaretto in Venice where Clay was in quarantine en route for home. The weather was 'foggy, wet, windy, horridly cold and wretched'. It is a letter which throws light on the recipient as well as the author.

> Dear Disraeli,
>
> Many returns of this day to you under kinder Gods than, I fear, rule your destiny at present. Between us we have contrived to stumble on all the thorns with which (as Mr Dickens, the Winchester Porter was wont poetically to observe) Venus guards her roses; for while you were cursing the greater evils I contrived to secure the minor viz a gleet from over exertion and crabs. The former I richly earned, and it wore itself out, the latter was quickly cured and I am in high cue for a real debauch in Venice . . .
>
> Yesterday being *my* birthday I drank our very good health . . . After dinner a capital batch of letters (yours included) arrived . . . I drank and drank again and read and re-read my letters until it became impossible to distinguish one correspondent from another. On reading what I thought was your hand-writing I found an exhortation to marry and settle, and when I took up, as I believed, a letter from my mother I read that 'Mercury had succeeded to Venus' – a most extraordinary communication from an elderly gentle-woman. This morning a splitting headache and two empty bottles informed me that for the first time in my life I had got *really* drunk solus cum solo.

Clay went on to give the latest news about Malta, where they had both been over a year before, and Venice, where Disraeli had hoped to go on his way back. In Malta the temporary Governor had had a fatal apoplectic seizure, occasioned 'by an anonymous letter to say his daughter had been rogered, who did not seem to me worth it'. As for Venice, the Consul there was a religious fanatic.

I fear Mr. Money and I shall not agree as he is Religious Mad. Giovanni says 'He keep very strict e si de people no go Sunday, sartainly de consul tink disa very bad people, e de consul preachy heself.' But as he has daughters I may furnish him with a text.

In fact it was not a daughter but the wife of the religious consul, whom Clay seduced.

Not surprisingly Disraeli's family deeply disapproved of this debauched young man. Sarah no doubt knew what Meredith thought of him. 'I am sure,' she wrote, in the tone of someone who is anything but sure, 'James Clay must be very much improved for you to make such a friend of him. How you come to be in a boat sailing with him on the Aegean Sea I cannot understand.' Half a century later in 1882 Sir Philip Rose, Disraeli's friend and solicitor, made a note on Clay's letter for Lord Rowton, who was Disraeli's executor:

There must be many more letters from this individual. The letter dated 21 December 1831 should be destroyed. The wife of the Consul at Venice mentioned in that letter is the lady whom Clay ran away with, soon afterwards, and who was the mother of all his children, tho' I believe he married her later in life, after her husband's death.

Clay was a thoroughly bad, unprincipled man. D's family had a horror of him, and dreaded his influence over D. He was at Brazenose [in fact Clay was at Balliol] with Meredith and was, I think, a contemporary of Ralph D. at Winchester, with whom he was intimate . . . It was a bad connexion for D. and one which gave him no pleasure in the retrospect, in after years, and he felt relieved that politics had to some extent divided them.

It is true that Clay, following his family tradition, became a Liberal MP (Hull 1847–53, Brighton 1857–73). He also became England's leading authority on whist and wrote an authoritative book on the subject. It is not clear that Sir Philip Rose was right in believing that Disraeli regretted the connection. There is the portrait

21

already mentioned, like that of the young Dorian Gray, at Hughenden, and the author of the notice of Clay in the *Dictionary of National Biography* says that Disraeli maintained their friendship to the end. When Clay was in his last illness in 1873 Disraeli called to enquire every day at his house.

Aware of the family's misgivings, Disraeli wrote somewhat defensively to Isaac on August 25 :

> To our surprise we find James Clay here, immensely improved and quite a hero. He has been here a month, and has already beat the whole garrison at Rackets, billiards and other wicked games, given lessons to their Prima Donna and seccatura'd [Disraeli meant 'annoyed'] the prima tenore. Really he has turned out a most agreeable personage and has had that advantage of society in which he had been deficient, and led a life which for splendid adventure wd beat any young gentleman's published in 3 vols pt 8 vo. Lord Burghersh wrote an opera for him and Lady Normanby a farce. He dished Prince Pignatelli at Billiards and diddled the Russian legation at Ecarté [a gambling game for two people with a Piquet pack. The ace curiously counts as the lowest court card].

It is doubtful whether these achievements reassured the Disraeli family. Sarah expressed her surprise when told that Benjamin and William were joining him as passengers (paid) on his yacht, and she observed of Lady Normanby that she had 'lost her reputation'.

The presence of Clay removed whatever restraining influence Meredith may have had on Disraeli. He now behaved with a flamboyance, conceit and affectation which did him no good, though he seems to have been wholly unaware of this in his letters. He told his father that there were several passengers in the original steam packet to Gibraltar who had preceded them to Malta. 'They have long been expecting your worship's offspring and have gained great fame in repeating his third rate stories at second hand : so in consequence of these messengers the Messiahship has answered and

I am received with branches of palm.' It may be doubted whether Disraeli made himself very popular though he certainly made himself notable. The young officers at Malta were addicted to rackets, billiards, cards and racing.

> To govern men you must either excel in their accomplishments – or despise them. Clay does one: I do the other, and we are equally popular [this may have been true in a sense]. Affectation tells here even better than wit. Yesterday at the racket court sitting in the gallery among strangers the ball entered, slightly struck me, and fell at my feet. I picked it up and observing a young rifleman excessively stiff I humbly requested him to forward its passage into the court, as I really had never thrown a ball in my life. This incident has been the general subject of conversation at all the messes today.

The Governor of Malta was Sir Frederick Ponsonby, whom Clay disliked because he had not received an invitation to dinner early enough in his stay. This 'so offended our friend who is excessively grand and talks of nothing but Burghersh, Normanby, Lady Williams and various Princes that he refused and is now in opposition'. The Governor, according to Disraeli, was said to be 'exceedingly exclusive in his conduct to his subjects', and it does seem true that the small English residential population headed by the Governor treated the Maltese rather as 'Anglo-Indians' treated the 'natives'. Malta had belonged to the Order of Knights Hospitallers from 1530 to 1798. In that year Napoleon seized it on his way to Egypt. The British captured it in 1800 and under the Treaty of Paris in 1814 it became a British possession. It was a key naval base and one of the principal links in the Mediterranean route to India.

Disraeli boldly called on the Governor and pulled out all the stops of his wit. 'I gave him no quarter, and at last made our nonchalant Governor roll on the sofa from his rissible [*sc.* risible] convulsions.' He did not linger, 'making it a rule always to leave a good impression', and departed along the Strada Reale where he got five invitations in quick succession to dinner from acquaintances. He called in at the Union Club, of which he was a temporary member (likewise of the Malta Sporting Club, 'which is a very exclusive establishment'). An invitation to dine with the Governor had arrived by the time he got home. 'Clay confesses my triumph is complete and unrivalled.'

Disraeli seems to have had a good time in Malta. He wrote to his brother on 17 September :

> Mashallah![1]
> Here I am smoking in an easy chair a Turkish pipe six feet long with an amber mouth piece and a porcelain bowl. What a revolution. But what if I tell you that I have not only become a smoker but the greatest smoker in Malta. The fact is I find it relieves the head and therefore give the Syriac, Latakia or Canastre[2] no quarter. Barrow who is here in the *Blonde* and a most knowing young Lieut who informed me the other night when drunk that he was sure to be made a captain in eighteen months ... presented me with the Turkish [and] has given me a Meerschaum, and Anstruther a most splendid Dresden green china set in most massy silver, an extremely valuable pipe.

His principal companions in Malta society were two army officers, George Liddell, a son of Lord Ravensworth, and Edmund Pery, later Lord Glentworth. The latter was to marry Eve Villebois, a sister of Disraeli's future mistress Lady Sykes – the only real love in his life. 'The society at Malta,' he loftily observed, 'is very superior indeed for a Colony.' He went on :

> A week ago I knew not what I would do. All is now settled. On Wednesday morning I quit this place where on the whole I have spent very agreeable hours, in the yacht which Clay has hired and in which he intends to turn pirate. The original plan was to have taken it together, but, as Meredith was

[1] An Arabic expression, 'What God wills must happen.'
[2] Different sorts of tobacco.

averse to the plan we have become his passengers at a fair rate and he drops us whenever and wherever we like. You should see me in the costume of a Greek pirate. A blood red shirt with silver studs as big as shillings[1], an immense scarf or girdle full of pistols and daggers, a red cap, red slippers, blue broad striped jacket and trousers. Excessively wicked !

Once more he sought to reassure his family about James Clay :

> Clay is immensely improved and a very agreeable companion indeed, with such a valet ! Giovanni by name. Byron died in his arms . . . Our yacht is of 55 tons, an excellent size for these seas, with a crew of 7 men. She is a very strong sea boat and bears the unpoetical name of Susan, which is a bore, but as we can't alter it we have painted it out.

A few days later they left Malta and sailed for Corfu. It was as well. There was a 'beauty' in Malta, 'very dangerous to the peace of your unhappy brother, but no more of that, and in a few weeks I shall be bounding, and perhaps sea sick upon the blue Aegean. Nothing like an emetic in these cases.' An *amour* that could be thus cured was not, one feels, very passionate.

[1] Meredith more cautiously and no doubt more accurately said 'sixpences'.

Chapter 2

Corfu and Albania
October 1830

I

The *Susan* arrived at Corfu early in October. The journey was 'stormy but not disagreeable', according to Disraeli, who added 'I like a sailor's life much, tho' it destroys the toilette and one never feels, or is indeed, clean.' The Ionian Islands, of which Corfu is the largest and most important, are the only part of modern Greece which never came under the rule of the Ottoman Turks. They belonged to Venice from 1401 to 1797 when, with the extinction of the Venetian Republic, they were ceded to France for a brief period. After various vicissitudes during the Napoleonic Wars, they became a British protectorate under the terms of the Treaty of Paris in 1815. But as soon as Greece became a nation state the Ionians clamoured for union. They would not be fobbed off by the constitutional reforms which Disraeli's great rival, Gladstone, recommended after his brief period as High Commissioner in 1858–9. In 1864 Palmerston's government ceded the islands to Greece; but a residual British influence has lingered on and cricket is still played there. It was thus in effect a British colony when Disraeli and his companions made their visit. 'This tho' a poor village', wrote Disraeli to his father on 10 October, 'is a most lovely island, offering all that you can expect from Grecian scenery, gleaming waters, woody isles, cypress, olive, vine, a clear sky and a warm sun.'

Though he only told of this in a letter to Austen and not to his family (who would have been horrified), Disraeli while in Malta had conceived the extraordinary plan of offering to join the Turkish army as a volunteer in its campaign to crush the Albanian revolt of 1830. It is hard to believe that he would have been a very effective officer.

There has been little biographical comment on this apparently serious resolve. Yet it was very odd, for he was running clean contrary to the trend of the world of radical youth to which he seemed to belong. Byron's espousal of the Greek rebellion against Turkish rule had fired the imagination of a whole generation – and Byron was one of Disraeli's heroes. Again and again in his words and life, the echo of Byron reverberates. He later wrote a novel based on Byron's life – *Venetia*, published in 1837. True, it is very bad, but that does not affect the paradox of a disciple of Byron adopting such an unByronic attitude in 1830. Disraeli, for whatever reason, took the view that the polyglot empire of the Sultan was a barrier against anarchy and barbarism. He was, all his life, totally unsympathetic to the spirit of nationalism which was the dominating force in his time. This lack of sympathy, along with his alleged indifference to 'liberty', was to be one of Gladstone's main charges against him. Certainly nobody was less willing than Disraeli to support the cause of 'nations struggling rightly to be free'.

Why Disraeli held this view is far from clear. It was no doubt a logical Tory attitude. The Duke of Wellington, who was Prime Minister from 1828 till November 1830, believed that the Porte was an indispensable bulwark against forces adverse to British interests, and one could cite many other examples. At this time even the Tsar, traditional enemy of the Sultan, believed that more harm would come from the disintegration than the continuance of the Turkish empire. But Disraeli was not a Tory, and, when he came to stand for Parliament soon after his return from his Grand Tour in a by-election at High Wycombe in 1832, he fought against the Whig candidate as an independent Radical. He took this line in two further unsuccessful contests. It was not till a by-election at Taunton in 1835 that he appeared as a committed Tory – though again without success.

His attitude to the Porte was not a foolish one. There were respectable arguments that the Greek war of independence was a cruel struggle between two equally barbaric forces and that the Greeks would have done better to infiltrate, colonize and take over the Ottoman empire peacefully, as they might well have done if events had gone slightly differently. Many of them already held high office and ran flourishing businesses. They constituted a quarter of the population of the empire. The cities with the largest numbers of Greeks at the beginning of the nineteenth century were Bucharest, Smyrna and Constantinople. Athens was a mere village. But it is unlikely that these considerations influenced Disraeli. From the beginning of his journey he had become ever more fascinated by the Mohammedan culture of the Mediterranean and Near East. One can see it in his reaction to the Moorish element in the architecture and tradition of Spain. He had fallen in love, as many Englishmen were to do after him, with the alien yet curiously hypnotic civilization of the Muslim world. Every further stage in his journey consolidated this strange love affair. The experiences of the roué and dandy of 1830–31 were to affect the attitude of the Prime Minister and statesman nearly half a century later at the Congress of Berlin.

The Albanian revolt had already been crushed by the time he reached Corfu. 'I am glad to say the Porte everywhere triumphant', he wrote. Instead of volunteering to fight on the side of the Grand Vizier, Reschid Mehmet Pasha, he volunteered to take a message to him from the 'Lord High', as he called him, i.e. the Lord High Commissioner of the Ionian Islands, General Sir Frederick Adam. Sir Frederick 'received me most courteously'. He entrusted Disraeli with an appropriate letter which he was to present to the Grand Vizier at Yanina, Meredith and Clay acting as his two aides-de-camp. As for his health, he wrote to his father in the same letter :

I continue much the same – still infirm but no longer destitute of hope. I wander in pursuit of health like the immortal exile in pursuit of that lost shore which is now almost glittering in my sight. Five years of my life have already been wasted, and sometimes I think my pilgrimage may be as long as that of Ulysses.

Adieu, my dearest friend. 1000 loves to all. I hope my letters duly arrived. I enumerated their respective dates in my last Malta letter. Write without ceasing.

The travellers arrived on 11 October at Prevesa, a few miles south-east of Corfu on the north-west coast of Greece. The mainland of the country had been convulsed for the last nine years by a revolutionary civil war of the utmost barbarity. It began in 1821 when the Greeks massacred with horrible cruelty most of the Turkish population. The crew of a Turkish corvette were individually roasted to death over slow fires on the beach of Hydra. The Sultan Mahmoud riposted with counter terror. The Patriarch of Constantinople who was supposed to have collective responsibility for his co-religionists was hanged at the gate of the Patriarchate. There were massacres of Greeks in Constantinople and Smyrna. The Turkish fleet, returning from one of its first cruises against the rebels, entered the harbour of Constantinople festooned with Greek prisoners hanging in their death agonies from every mast and bowsprit.

The conflict within Greece was not so much one of race or nationalism, as of fanatical religious bigotry. But the Europeanized Greeks who supported the revolt from outside saw it in terms of 'liberty', self-government, the nation state and the usual slogans of 'progressive' thought current since the French Revolution. The Greek cause was supported in England by the kind of committee of high-minded 'do-gooders' familiar from that day to this. They were Whigs or Radicals almost to a man, the only exception being an eccentric Tory clergyman, Thomas Hughes, who believed on religious principle that all Turks should be exterminated. Inevitably the name of the arch-panjandrum of advanced radicalism, Jeremy Bentham, was invoked, and the aged philosopher wrote long homilies on constitutionalism for the benefit of the savage war lords and robber chieftains who dominated the Greek Provisional Government. Perhaps Disraeli's pro-Turk feelings stemmed less from dislike of the Greeks than dislike of the sort of people who supported them in England.

The Sultan, like the rulers of modern Russia surveying Poland, sensed that any flicker of nationalism, however incomprehensible the principle might be to his own government, or even to the indigenous Greeks themselves, would, if successful, be a fatal precedent for other areas of his multi-racial empire. This partly explains the brutality of Turkish measures against an equally brutal revolution. Turkish repression was aided by the factionalism and incompetence of the European Philhellenes and the Greeks themselves. Curiously, of all the Philhellene figures, Byron, the most romanticized, was also the most realistic. Though hopelessly indecisive as a military commander, he saw through the cant, hypocrisy and corruption which surrounded him before his death at Missolonghi in April 1824.

By 1827 the Greek revolution was about to collapse. The Sultan three years earlier had invoked the aid of his formidable and virtually independent vassal, Mehemet Ali, the Albanian adventurer who, after a series of military triumphs, tortuous intrigues and hideous murders, had become Pasha of Egypt. His son, Ibrahim, with a powerful fleet and a disciplined army would have crushed the revolt but for an accident. Already, Missolonghi, to the horror of the Byronmanes, had been captured in April 1826 and the usual atrocities had followed. A year later the Acropolis was taken. The Greek cause appeared to be doomed. Very late in the day the British, French and Russian governments concluded a pact, the Treaty of London, under which they agreed to press for an armistice and to support their pressure by a naval demonstration in the Aegean. The Turks, on the verge of victory, had no intention of agreeing, nor had the Allies of using force to compel them. But a series of muddles and misunderstandings led on 20 October 1827 to an accidental outbreak of hostilities between the Turkish and Allied fleets in the bay of Navarino on the south-west coast of the Morea. The Turkish fleet was obliterated in this last great naval battle under sail. The 'untoward incident', as it was described with masterly understatement in the King's Speech in 1828, transformed the situation. Sea power was the key to Ibrahim's strategy. The Greeks were saved, despite their exertions and example.

2

Neither the status nor frontiers of the new Greece had been settled when Disraeli and his friends landed at Prevesa. The Turks, thanks to Navarino, had failed to reconquer the south and the Morea, but they were in control of Epirus, then a mixed Greek-Albanian border-land, and also of Macedonia. These did not become a part of Greece till 1913. Disraeli's long letter to his father from Prevesa on 25 October describing his visit to Yanina is one of his best. The travellers were well treated by the Consul General at Prevesa, 'Mr Meyer . . . a gentleman of the old school . . . He insists upon us dining with him every night and, what is remarkable, produces a cuisine which wd not be despicable in London, but in this savage land of anarchy is indeed as surprising as it is agreeable.'

But they could not linger. The movements of the Grand Vizier were uncertain and unpredictable. The *Susan* took them north to Salora and, with a company of armed horsemen, they set off for Arta, a few miles inland. Apart from a recently rebuilt house belonging to the Consulate and made ready for their accommodation, they found the place in ruins, but Disraeli was fascinated to hear for the first time the *muezzin* from the minaret, 'a ceremony which is highly affecting, when performed, as it usually is, by a rich and powerful voice'. Next day they called on the Governor, Kalio Bey, a rich Albanian grandee who had prudently kept in with the Porte throughout his career, whereas nearly all the rest of the Albanian aristocracy were implicated in the revolt. 'I cannot describe to you the awe with which I first entered the divan[1] of a Great Turk, or the curious feelings with which for the first time in my life I found myself squatting on the right hand of a Bey smoking an amber mouthed chibooque, drinking coffee and paying him compliments through an interpreter.' The Bey furnished the party with two Albanian armed guards and two Turkish guides to show them the way to Yanina where the Grand Vizier was ensconced, after crushing the rebellion with fire and slaughter in the usual Turkish style. The journey proved longer than they expected and two hours before sunset they found themselves at a military post in the Pindus mountains, 'as big as a Gothic castle'. There they found a young Bey to whom Kalio had given them a letter of introduction, but unfortunately he could not understand Tita's Greek.

> What was to be done ! We could not go on, as there was not an inhabited place before Yanina and here were we sitting before Sunset, on the same Divan with our host who had entered the place to receive us, and would not leave the room while we were there, without the power of communicating an idea. We were in despair, and we were also very hungry, and could not therefore in the course of an hour or two plead fatigue as an excuse for sleep, for we were ravenous, and anxious to know what prospect of food existed in this wild and desolate mansion.

So they decided to smoke, but one could not go on smoking for ever, exchanging pipes as a compliment and pressing hand to heart as a signal of gratitude. Disraeli had the bad luck to sit next to the Bey and thus 'had the onus of mute attention'. Clay characteristically thought it might be a good idea to play Ecarté with a solemn expression as if they were at their devotions, but just as they were

[1] Divan is a Persian word which meant a council of state and by transference, the hall or chamber where the council was held. This is the sense in which Disraeli uses it here. Later in the same letter he uses the word in its normal English sense of a sort of sofa or couch.

about to begin one of them remembered that they had some brandy. If they offered it to their host as an aperitif, 'it might be a hint for what should follow so vehement a schnaps'.

> Mashallah! had the effect only taken place 1830 years ago, instead of in the present age of scepticism, it would have been instantly voted a first rate miracle. Our mild friend drank it in coffee cups. By the time that Meredith had returned, who had left the house on pretence of shooting, Clay, our host and myself had despatched a bottle of brandy in quicker time and fairer proportions than I ever did a bottle of Burgundy and were extremely gay. Then he would drink again with Meredith and ordered some figs, talking I must tell you all the time, indulging in the most graceful pantomime, examining our pistols, offering us his own golden ones for our inspection, and finally – making out Giovanni's Greek enough to misunderstand most ludicrously every observation we communicated.

All this took place in a mood of good humour. But there was no sign of food other than 'the dry round unsugary fig' which, so Disraeli alleged, merely whetted an already ravenous appetite. Finally Tita managed to convey that the travellers wanted bread. The Bey bowed and said ' "leave it to me, take no thought" '. Still nothing happened.

> We prepared ourselves for hungry dreams, when to our great delight a most capital supper was brought in accompanied to our great horror by – wine. We ate – we drank in a manner I never recollect – the wine was not bad, but if it had been poison, we must drink, it was such a compliment for a Moslemin, we quaffed it in rivers – the Bey called for the Brandy – we drank it all – the room turned round, the wild attendants who sat at our feet seemed dancing in strange and fantastic whirls, the Bey shook hands with me, he shouted English – I Greek –'very good' he had caught up from us – 'kalo, kalo,' was my rejoinder.

By this time the whole party was extremely drunk. Disraeli smacked the Bey on the back, but after that remembered no more. He woke up in the middle of the night and found that he had been sleeping on the Divan, 'rolled up in its sacred carpet', the Bey having 'wisely reeled to the fire'.

> The thirst I felt was like that of Dives – all were sleeping except two, who kept up during the night the great wood fire. I rose, lightly stepping over my sleeping companions, and the shining arms that here and there informed me that the dark mass wrapped up in a capote was a human being. I found Abraham's bosom in a flagon of water. I think I must have drank a Gallon of the draught. I looked at the wood fire, and thought of the blazing blocks in the Hall at Bradenham, asked myself whether I was indeed in the mountain fastness of an Albanian chief, and shrugging my shoulders, went to sleep and woke without a headache.
>
> We left our jolly host with regret. I gave him my pipe as a memorial of having got tipsey together.

Next day the party continued on their journey to Yanina. The landscape was one of desolation, 'villages in ruins and perfectly uninhabited, caravanserais deserted, fortresses raised to the ground, olive woods burnt up'. At last they came to Yanina, 'once if not the largest, one of the most prosperous and most brilliant in the Turkish dominions'. At a distance it still looked impressive, but 'I soon found that all the preceding desolation had only been preparative to the vast scene of destruction now before me . . . Ruined houses, mosques with their tower only standing, streets utterly erased.' There were square miles of ruin 'as if a swarm of locusts had had the power of desolating the works of man as well as God'. But in other respects the city seemed anything but sad.

> At this moment a swarming population, arrayed in every possible and fanciful costume, buzzed and bustled in all directions. As we passed on, and you can easily believe, not unobserved, where no '*mylords Ingles*' (as regular a word

among the Turks as the French and Italians) had been seen for more than nine years, a thousand objects attracted my restless attention and roving eye. Every thing was so strange and splendid, that for a moment I forgot that this was an extraordinary scene even for the East, and gave up my fancy to a full credulity in the now obsolete magnificence of Oriental life. Military chieftains clothed in the most brilliant colours, and most showy furs, and attended by a cortege of officers equally splendid, continually passed us.

The Albanian costume was 'inexhaustible'. Disraeli's first day in 'Turkey' – the word being an interesting reminder of the status of 'Greece' – evoked all that he had read and thought about that strange, alien, yet to Disraeli fascinating, empire. Yanina 'brought before me all the popular characteristics of which I had read, and which, I expected, I might occasionally see during a prolonged residence'. He saw a series of curiously exotic spectacles – 'a Turkish Scheik in his entirely green vestments, a Scribe with his writing materials in his girdle and a little old Greek physician' who claimed to speak English on the strength of being able to count nine on his fingers.

Suddenly a strange, wild, unearthly drum is heard, and at the end of the street a huge camel, to me it seemed as large as an elephant, with a slave sitting crosslegged on its neck and playing an immense kettle drum, appears and is the first of an apparently interminable procession of his Arabian brethren. The camels were very large, they moved slowly, and were many in number – I should think there might have been between 60 and 100 one by one. It was an imposing sight – all immediately hustled out of the way of the Caravan and seemed to shrink under the sound of the wild drum. This procession bore corn for the Vizier's troops encamped without the wall.

In due course they were presented by the Austrian Consul to the Grand Vizier, Reschid Mehmet Pasha himself, in his fortress palace and Disraeli handed the High Commissioner's letter to him. There was a host of suppliants in his ante-chamber who looked as if they would wait for ever, but the English party went ahead of them all.

Here squatted up in a corner of the large divan I bowed with all the nonchalance of St. James St. to a little, ferocious looking, shrivelled, careworn man, plainly dressed with a brow covered with wrinkles, and a countenance clouded with anxiety and thought. I [had] entered the shedlike Divan of the kind and comparatively insignificant Kalio Bey with a feeling of awe. I seated myself on the Divan of the Grand Vizier, who as the Austrian Consul observed, has destroyed, in the course of the last three months *not* in war, 'upwards of four thousand of my acquaintance', with the self-possession of a morning call.

Some compliments now passed between us, and pipes and coffee were then brought; then his Highness waved his hand and in an instant the chamber was cleared. Our conversation I need not repeat. We congratulated him on the pacification of Albania. He rejoined that the peace of the world was his only object and the happiness of mankind his only wish; this went on for the usual time. He asked us no questions about ourselves or our country as the other Turks did but seemed quite overwhelmed with business, moody and anxious. While we were with him, three separate Tartars arrived with dispatches. What a life! and what a slight chance for the gentlemen in the ante chamber.

The Albanian rebellion had been suppressed with a degree of duplicity and ruthlessness which even surpassed the normal behaviour of the Turkish authorities on these occasions. The massacre of the Albanian Beys was long remembered as a notable atrocity. Eventually the travellers took leave of the Grand Vizier and paid a visit to his son,

Amin Pacha, a youth of eighteen, but who looks ten years older and who is Pacha of Yanina. He is the very reverse of his father – incapable in affairs, refined in his manners, plunged in debauchery and magnificent in dress. Covered with gold and diamonds he bowed to us with the ease of a Duke of Devonshire and said the English were the most polished of nations.

In a rather briefer letter to Benjamin Austen, Disraeli in reference to his audience with the Grand Vizier speaks of 'the delight of being made much of by a man who was daily decapitating half the Province'.

They were in Yanina for a week 'and', as he wrote to Austen, 'crammed ourselves with sweetmeats. Every evening dancers and singers were sent to our quarters by the Vizier or some Pasha.' By 25 October they were back in Prevesa. 'I write to you [Isaac D'Israeli] from that Ambracian Gulph where the soft Triumvir gained more glory by defeat than attends the victory of harsher warriors' – Disraeli's way of saying that he was at the place of the great naval battle of Actium, in which Octavian defeated Anthony and Cleopatra. He went on :

The dying glory of a Grecian eve bathes with warm light a thousand promontories, and gentle bays, and infinite undulations of purple outline. Before me is Olympus, whose austere peak glitters yet in the sun : a bend of the land alone hides from me the islands of Ulysses and Sappho. When I gaze upon this scene I remember the barbaric splendor and turbulent existence, which I have just quitted, with disgust. I recur to the feelings in the indulgence of which I can alone find happiness and from which an inexorable destiny seems resolved to shut me out.

Despite his disgust at 'the barbaric splendor' of Yanina, the episode left a lasting imprint on his mind. Passages are repeated almost word for word from his letters, which he no doubt recovered from the family, in chapters X to XV in Part V of *Contarini Fleming*, his 'Psychological Auto-Biography', as he called it. But the hero there is allowed to do what the course of events denied to Disraeli – participate on the Grand Vizier's side in the battle of Monastir or Bitoglia against the forces of the Pasha of Scutari.

> The Vizier gave orders for a general charge and pursuit, and in a few minutes I was dashing over the hills in rapid chase of all I could catch, cutting, firing and shouting, and quite persuaded that a battle, after all, is the most delightful pastime in the world.

> The masses still charging, the groups demanding quarter, the single horseman bounding over the hills the wild scared steeds without a rider, snorting and plunging, the dense smoke clearing away, the bright arms and figures flashing ever and anon in the moving obscurity, the wild shouts, the strange and horrible spectacles, the solitary shots and shrieks now heard in the decreasing uproar and the general feeling of energy and peril, and triumph – it was all wonderful and a glorious moment in existence.

Contarini returns to his tent, drinks 'a flask of Zitza wine' at a draught and experiences 'the highest sensual pleasure'. He then rides by moonlight over the field of battle to see the victorious Redschid seated on a carpet in a cypress grove, who gives him 'the pipe of honour from his own lips'.

Chapter 3

Greece and Constantinople

October 1830 – January 1831

I

The travellers now sailed for Athens. By 1830 the fighting in Morea, Hellas and Thessaly had come to an end. The Turks, distracted by the Russian seizure, following Navarino, of the Principalities of Moldavia and Wallachia (the core of modern Rumania), were in no position to reconquer the southern part of Greece. The Principalities in 1829 became, under the Treaty of Adrianople, in all but name Russian vassal states. In Morea a French expeditionary force landed in 1828, and in the same year Admiral Codrington, the British commander at Navarino, negotiated a convention under which Ibrahim, increasingly aware of the growing risk of remaining, peacefully withdrew his army to Egypt. There only remained the question of settling the juridical status and boundaries of a new independent Greek state guaranteed by the three great powers. This was not achieved till after the refusal of the throne in 1830 by Leopold of Coburg (who got Belgium instead) and the assassination in October 1831 of Capodistria, the remarkable Corfu Greek who first became Foreign Minister of Russia and then President of the Provisional Greek government. In May 1832 King Louis of Bavaria accepted the uneasy crown on behalf of his seventeen-year-old second son, Prince Otto, and modern Greece came into being. The decision turned out to be a disaster, though this was hardly predictable at the time. Many months earlier Disraeli had returned to England, and he was never to be in those parts again.

The *Susan* sailed in a leisurely way along the south-west coast of

Hellas and Morea in perfect weather, much warmer than normal for the season. Pirates were the only threat.

> We sailed from Prevesa through the remaining Ionian islands among which was Zante, preeminent in beauty ; indeed they say none of the Cyclades are to be compared to it with its olive trees touching the waves, and its shores undulating in every possible variety. For about a fortnight we were for ever sailing on a summer sea, always within two or three miles of the coast and touching at every island or harbour that invited. A cloudless sky, a summer atmosphere, and sunsets like the neck of a dove, completed all the enjoyment which I anticipated from roving in a Grecian sea. We were obliged however to keep a sharp look out for Pirates, who are all about again – we exercised the crew every day with muskets, and their encreasing prowess, and our own pistol exercise, kept up our courage.

Rather surprisingly they did not put in at Missolonghi, although it was almost on their route. Disraeli wrote to Austen :

> We were a week at the scene of Codrington's bloody blunder, Navarino, a superb, perhaps unrivalled harbour, with the celebrated Sphacteria on one side and old Pylos on the other. Here we found the French in all their glory. They have already covered the scene of Spartan suffering with cafés and billiard rooms and make daily picnics to the grotto of Nestor. Navarino looks greatly like a French village. From Navarino after visiting Modon and sailing by the bay of Coron, the Promontory of Malea, Cerigo, a beautiful island, we reached Napoli.

The port, which Disraeli thus confusingly describes and from which he was writing the letter just quoted, is usually known as Nauplia or Nauplion. It was a flourishing place and had been for a time the capital of the Provisional Government. The trio made it a base for excursions to Argos, Mycenae and Corinth – the last-named, he told

Disraeli's father, Isaac D'Israeli, in 1797. Highly regarded as a writer and man-of-letters, Isaac was the recipient of most of his son's Home Letters.

Disraeli's only sister, Sarah, in 1828. Apart from Isaac, she was the only member of the family who had something of Benjamin's mental ability.

The 'author of *Vivian Grey*', depicted as a fashionable dandy, in the 1830s.
The long pipe on the sofa is a reminder of Disraeli's eastern Tour.

James Clay. Disraeli's family deeply disapproved of this rich, young debauchee on whose yacht Disraeli sailed from Malta onwards.

Byron in Albanian dress.

Giovanni Battista Falcieri, or 'Tita', Byron's one-time gondolier and manservant. After the Tour, Disraeli found Tita a home at Bradenham Manor (where this portrait was drawn in 1836) and later, after Isaac D'Israeli's death, got him the post of Chief Messenger at the India Office.

Corfu, around the time of Disraeli's visit.

Yanina.

his father, 'a scene which, both for beauty and associations will not easily be forgotten'. Writing to Austen, he said :

> I am quite a Turk, wear a turban, smoke a pipe six feet long and squat on a divan. Mehmet Pasha [the Grand Vizier] told me that he did not think I was an Englishman because I walked *so slow*. In fact I find the habits of this calm and luxurious people entirely agree with my own preconceived opinions of propriety, and I detest the Greeks more than ever. I do not find mere travelling on the whole very expensive, but I am ruined by my wardrobe . . . When I was presented to the Grand Vizier I made up such a costume from my heterogeneous wardrobe that the Turks who are mad on the subject of dress were utterly astounded . . . Nothing would persuade the Greeks that we were not come about the new King and I really believe that if I had 25,000 L to throw away I might increase my headache by wearing a crown.

Disraeli was no doubt joking. Even the most desperate group of Greek politicians would scarcely have considered him in this light at this time, especially if they knew his opinion of themselves. But odd things were to happen about the crown of Greece. When it became vacant thirty years later the names of Gladstone, Bulwer-Lytton and Lord Stanley, the 14th Earl of Derby's heir, were considered (among a host of others) by various Greek groups. Disraeli wrote, perhaps with nostalgic memories, 'It is a dazzling adventure for the House of Stanley but they are not an imaginative race, and, I fancy, they will prefer Knowsley to the Parthenon and Lancashire to the Attic plain'.

From Nauplia they sailed for the Piraeus, about six miles from Athens. The Greeks had driven out the Turks in 1822 but it had been recaptured four years later, and the Turks had seized the Acropolis in 1827 :

> I climbed a small hill forming a side of the harbour. From it I looked upon an immense plain covered with olive woods and skirted by mountains. Some isolated hills rise at a distance from the bounding ridge. On one of these I gazed upon a

magnificent temple bathed in the sunset; at the foot of the hill was a walled city of considerable dimensions in front of which was a Doric temple apparently quite perfect. The violet sunset, and today the tint was peculiarly vivid, threw over this scene a coloring becoming its beauty, and, if possible, increasing its delicate character. The city was Athens, but independent of all reminiscences, I never witnessed anything so truly beautiful, and I have seen a great deal.

We were fortunate. The Acropolis which has been shut for nine years was open to us, the first Englishmen. Athens is still in the power of the Turks, but the Grecian commission to receive it arrived a short time before us. When we entered the city we found every house roofless, but really before the war, modern Athens must have been no common town. The ancient remains have been respected. The Parthenon and the other temples which are in the Acropolis, have necessarily suffered during the siege, but the injury is only in the detail ; the general effect is not marred. We saw hundreds of shells and balls lying among the ruins. The temple of Theseus looks at a short distance, as if it were just finished by Pericles. Gropius, a well known character, was the only civilised being in this almost uninhabited town, and was our excellent Cicerone.

Disraeli and his companions then set out on an excursion in the country to visit Marathon and other places. He told his father :

I can give you no idea of the severe hardship and privation of present Grecian travel. Happy are we to get a shed for nightly shelter, and never have been fortunate enough to find one not swarming with vermin. My sufferings in this way are great, and so are poor Clay's, but Meredith escapes. Our food must not be quarrelled with, for we lived for a week on the wild boar of Pentelicus, and the honey of Hymettus, both very good; and I do not care for privation in this respect, as I have always got my pipe, but the want of sleep from vermin, and literally I did not sleep a wink the whole time I was out, is very bad, as it unfits you for daily exertion.

We found a wild boar just killed at a little village and purchased half of it – but it is not as good as Bradenham pork.

It was time to move. They were by now waiting for a south-west wind to take them on the next leg of the journey. After two days at Aegina, the island south of the Piraeus, a favourable wind blew up and they were off for Constantinople, where they arrived on 10 December.

We have had a most splendid view of Sunium: its columns looked like undriven snow, and are now among the clustering Cyclades – sixteen islands in sight, and we are making our course east among the heart of them: our passage promises wonderfully.

We have reached the Dardanelles – a capital passage. What a road to a great city – narrower and much longer than the straits of Gibraltar, but not with such sublime shores. Asia and Europe look more kindly on each other, than Europe and her more sultry sister.

The breeze has again sprung up. We have yet one hundred and thirty miles to Constantinople.

It is near sunset and Const. is in full sight ; it baffles all description, tho' so often described ; an immense mass of buildings, cupolas, cypress groves and minarets. I feel an excitement, which I thought was dead.

2

Disraeli was to stay in Constantinople for some six weeks. He was fascinated by the sights and sounds of the city and by the character of Turkish rule. For the Ottoman Empire was, on any view, a most extraordinary institution. That it was an unbridled despotism is not surprising. Although 1830 was a year of revolutions, few succeeded and most of Europe remained under the rule of autocracies of one sort or another, apart from Britain, France and the Low Countries. That the Sultanate was extremely inefficient is also not surprising. Autocracies, contrary to popular belief, are far less competent than liberal democracies. One has only to look at the contrast between the countries east and west of the Iron Curtain today, to see the point. What was remarkable about the Ottoman Empire was its sheer tenacity and power of survival, for the Turks, unlike the other barbarian invaders of Europe, had never either assimilated or been assimilated by the peoples they had conquered. Between their European subjects and them there was the impenetrable barrier of creed. In the nineteenth century, outside observers came to believe that a religion so obscurantist, as they thought Islam to be, must gradually decline into an eccentric anachronism, under the solvent effects of Christianity on the one hand and secularism on the other. This was an optimistic view, as events in Iran if nowhere else have recently shown. The gulf between the Turks, an armed Muslim camp in a conquered country, and their Christian subjects was never bridged.

There was both acute religious and acute nationalist dissent, the two being closely, but by no means always or indissolubly, connected. Moreover the Sultan ruled over a vast sprawling empire which in 1800 covered in Europe modern Rumania, Bulgaria, much of modern Yugoslavia and the whole of Greece; in northern Africa – Algeria, Tunisia, Libya and Egypt; in Asia – Turkey, Syria, Palestine, Iraq, the Hejaz and Aden. Communications from Constantinople were infinitely slow. The Sultans, once the commanders of an army of expansion, had become the feeble products of a series of palace revolutions, made and unmade by the Janissaries, an army corps, like the Roman Pretorian Guards useless in the art of war, but skilled in that of insurrection. The governors of the remoter provinces often turned themselves into independent satraps and were left alone, as long as suitable tribute, along with baskets of heads and salted ears, were sent to Constantinople from time to time to assure the Sultan that law and order prevailed. Ali Pasha, 'the Lion of Yanina', who built the fortress palace in which Disraeli bowed to the Grand Vizier, at one time held the whole balance of power in the Balkans – till he actually attempted to assassinate one of the Sultan's household and, after two years of ferocious fighting was defeated, betrayed and murdered in 1822. Even more striking was the case of Mehemet Ali, the Albanian soldier of fortune already mentioned. He was confirmed as Pasha of Egypt in 1806 and in 1811 assured himself of a virtually independent position by massacring in circumstances of extreme treachery in Cairo the Mameluke Beys, the descendants of emancipated, largely Circassian, slaves who had constituted the Egyptian ruling class for several hundred years. In 1826 by a similar but even more bloody *coup* the Sultan Mahmoud II exterminated the Janissaries in Constantinople.

Fanatical, religious and national feuds, over-mighty subjects, poverty, military incompetence, perpetual battles about the succession – how did the regime survive? It had two assets. One was the problem of what should replace it. On this the European great powers were far from clear. Britain regarded Turkey as a bulwark against a Russian assault (highly improbable though it now seems) on the route to

India. The Habsburg Empire was as vulnerable to nationalism as the Ottomans and had a vested interest in the status quo. France saw nothing obvious to be gained by its disappearance. The Russians themselves perceived advantages in cautious infiltration rather than total destruction which might produce, and in the end did produce, independent Christian states as hostile to Russia as their inhabitants had previously been to the Sublime Porte.

More important than any of these considerations was something which Disraeli intuitively recognized – the ideological solidarity of the governing class. The Ottoman Turks never had a flicker of doubt about the sanctity and legitimacy of the regime. The expediency of ruthless repression might at times be a subject for argument, the morality and propriety never. This confident ideology, like that of the modern rulers of Russia, did not exclude the possibility of fear, panic and sheer miscalculation leading to disastrous decisions. But it meant that, unlike the French aristocracy before the Revolution or the British middle class before the decolonization of India and Africa, the Ottomans suffered from no sense of guilt; they never questioned the ethics of the system. Mahmoud II was a 'reforming' Sultan but only in the sense that he intended, for example by murdering the Janissaries, to make the system more efficient for its basic purpose – the prevention of anarchy and the preservation of Islam. This single-mindedness was a great source of strength. It could be, indeed was in the end, overcome by *force majeure*, but people had been talking of the 'sick man of Europe' and prophesying death from the eighteenth century on. It was not till the 1914–18 war, the greatest military convulsion in world history, that the invalid finally succumbed.

On arrival at Constantinople Disraeli was disappointed to find that a friend at the embassy, George Seymour, had left to become Minister in Florence, but the loss turned out to be more than counter-balanced by the affability of the ambassador, Sir Robert Gordon. He was a younger brother of Lord Aberdeen, who had just ceased to be Foreign Secretary and was in due course to become Prime Minister. Gordon, despite being a first-cousin of Byron, was very pro-Turk and strongly anti-Greek. He was not a very efficient ambassador and was soon pushed out by Palmerston. His only claim to fame is that when he retired some years later he bought Balmoral (the original shooting lodge), leaving it on his death in 1847 to his brother, from whom the Prince Consort was first to lease and then buy it. But whatever his diplomatic defects he was most hospitable to Disraeli, Clay and Meredith. They could dine with him at 'the Palace', i.e. the embassy, whenever they wanted, as long as they sent a message in the morning ; he introduced them to the other ambassadors and he invited them to every picnic. Disraeli wrote to his father on 11 January 1831 :

> I can give a favourable bulletin of my health which continues improving: in fact I hope the early spring will return me to Bradenham in very different plight to that in which I left it. I can assure you that I sigh to return altho' in very agreeable company; but I have seen and done enough in this way, and a mingled picture of domestic enjoyment and fresh butter, from both of which I have been so long estranged daily flits across my fancy.
>
> Meredith quit us to our great regret a fortnight ago, as he always intended, and is now wandering among the Bithynian mountains, which are remarkable for being more devoid of interest than any hills in existence. We anticipate meeting him at Smyrna, and if so, may probably find him not disinclined to renounce his intentions of being a discoverer.

One of Disraeli's first activities was to make himself up to date with politics by perusing the back numbers of *Galignani's Messenger* – an English news sheet widely circulated in the capitals of Europe. Much had happened. There was the bloodless July revolution in Paris, the Belgian uprising against the House of Orange in September, the Polish rebellion against Russia in November. In England the death of George IV produced a general election in late July and early August. It left the balance of parties much as before, but it was a disappointment to the Tories who had expected to gain. On November 2 in the debate on the Address in the House of Lords, Wellington made a speech so hostile to parliamentary reform that it brought down his government a few days later. The public uproar was such that the Cabinet had to cancel their acceptances of the Guildhall Banquet on 9 November. Defeated on 15 November, the Duke resigned next day. Earl Grey was appointed as Prime Minister and the Whigs were to dominate the political scene for the next eleven years. Among the odder appointments to the new Cabinet was Henry Brougham, the arch-radical, who accepted amidst general laughter the Lord Chancellorship and a peerage. 'What a confusion ! What a capital Pantomime,' wrote Disraeli to Isaac, 'Lord Mayor's Day, or Harlequin Brougham !' And he repeated the phrase to at least two other correspondents. He evidently had political ambitions before he set off on his tour. The death of the King and the ensuing crisis over the Reform Bill resulted in two general elections while he was away. Had he been at home, he would probably have made an effort to stand, but there is no reason to believe that he would have been more or less successful then than he was later.

As for his surroundings, 'Description is an acknowledged bore so I leave Constantinople to your imagination', he wrote to his father – a statement which naturally in no way inhibited him from describing the city at some length:

> Cypress groves and mosquish domes, masses of habitations grouped on gentle acclivities rising out of the waters, millions of minarets, a sea, like a river, covered with innumerable long, thin, boats, as swift as gondolas, and far more gay, being carved and gilt – all these and this, when filled with a swarming population in rich and brilliant and various costume, will afford you a more lively, and certainly not a more incorrect, idea than, half a dozen pages worthy of Horace Smith. There are two things here which cannot be conceived without inspection – the Bosphorus and the Bazaar. Conceive the Ocean a stream not broader than the Thames at Gravesend, with shores with all the variety and beauty of the Rhine, covered with palaces, mosques, villages, groves of cypress and

woods of Spanish chestnut. The view of the Euxine at the end
is the most sublime thing I can remember.

Disraeli dwelt on the delights of the Bazaar. It was like the Burlington
Arcade or similar places in Paris, but far larger, 'perhaps a square mile
of these arcades intersecting each other in all directions and full of
every product of the Empire from diamonds to dates'. He was
enthusiastic about the magnificence and variety of the goods on
display, 'the whole nation of shopkeepers all in different national
dress' :

> Here every people have a characteristic costume. Turks,
> Greeks, Jews and Armenians are the staple population; the
> latter seem to predominate. The Armenians wear round and
> very unbecoming black caps and robes, the Jews a black hat
> wreathed with a white handkerchief, the Greeks black tur-
> bans. The Turks indulge in all combinations of costume. The
> meanest merchant in the Bazaar looks like a Sultan in an
> Eastern fairy tale. This is mainly to be ascribed to the marvel-
> lous brilliancy of their dyes, which is one of the most remark-
> able circumstances in their social life, and which never has
> been explained to me. A common pair of slippers that you
> purchase in the street is tinged of a vermilion or a lake so
> extraordinary, that I can compare their color to nothing but
> the warmest beam of a southern sunset.

Disraeli was not presented to the Sultan but saw him several times.
'He affects all the affable activity of a European Prince, mixes with his
subjects, interferes in all their pursuits and taxes them most unmerci-
fully.' Ever sharp on clothes, Disraeli noted that the Sultan dressed
like a European 'and all the young men have adopted the fashion. You
see the young Turks in uniforms which would not disgrace one of our
cavalry regiments, and lounging with all the idleness of royal
illegitimates. It is on the rising generation that the Sultan depends,
and if one may form an opinion, not in vain.' Mahmoud II, who
reigned from 1808 to 1839, was a man of ability who endeavoured to

55

restore the tottering fortunes of the Ottoman Empire and to some extent succeeded.

> After all his defeats, he has now sixty thousand regular infantry excellently appointed and well disciplined. They are certainly not to be compared to the French or English line – but they would as certainly beat the Spanish or the Dutch, and many think with fair play, the Russians. Fair play their monarch certainly had not during the last campaign. Its secret history would not now interest, but it was by other means than military prowess that the Muscovites advanced so successfully. The Sultan had to struggle against an unprecedented conspiracy the whole time, and the morning that Adrianople was treacherously delivered up, the streets of Stamboul were filled with the dead bodies of detected traitors.

All his life Disraeli was a convinced adherent of the conspiracy theory of history. He was himself an adept at intrigue, and he detected this capacity in everyone else. Secret societies, plots, manoeuvres, treachery, double dealing – these were to him the essence of war and politics. There is in fact no reason to believe that the Russians defeated the Ottoman armies otherwise than by straightforward military superiority.

Disraeli ended his letter from Constantinople :

> I have been inside a Mosque – Suleimana, which is nearly as large and far more beautiful than Sophia.
> The most wonderful thing here are the burial grounds – but it is vain to write. I must return, if only to save you from reading these stupid letters. I expect in ten days to be in Egypt as the wind is most favourable. From that country I shall return to Malta and then to Naples at least these are my plans which may probably not be executed. I wish to get back for Bradenham races, but very much fear I shall not, unless I can somehow or other shuffle quarantine which is a month or six weeks from these awful parts.

Esperons !

Tell Ralph we are very gay here, nothing but masquerade balls and diplomatic dinners. The Ambassador has introduced us everywhere. We had the most rollicking week at the Palace, with romping of the most horrible description, and things called 'games of forfeits'. Gordon, out of the purest malice, made me tumble over head and heels! Can you conceive anything more dreadful? There are only two attachés here: Villiers, a very clever and agreeable person; and Buchanan, a good fellow.

Disraeli clearly enjoyed every moment of his stay in Constantinople. On 27 December he wrote to Bulwer-Lytton:

I confess to you that my Turkish prejudices are very much confirmed by my residence in Turkey. The life of this people greatly accords with my taste which is naturally somewhat indolent and melancholy. And I do not think it would disgust you. To repose on voluptuous ottomans and smoke superb pipes, daily to indulge in the luxury of a bath which requires half a dozen attendants for its perfection; to court the air in a carved caique, by shores which are a perpetual scene; this is, I think, a far more sensible life than all the bustle of clubs, all the boring of drawing rooms and all the coarse vulgarity of our political controversies . . . I mend slowly but mend. The seasons have greatly favoured me. Continued heat. And even here, where the winter is proverbially cold, there is a summer sky.

There can be no doubt that Disraeli's experiences in the domains or former domains of the Sultan had a lasting influence on his opinions. Again and again in his novels and correspondence one finds him half jesting at the parliamentary institutions through which he was to rise to eminence. He was not at heart a believer in liberty, or representative government ('fatal drollery', he described it). He appreciated that these were ineradicable parts of English political life, and he was fully prepared to play the game according to the rules and to take good care to know the rules extremely well. In the course of time he would hold his own in this arena with anyone, Russell, Palmerston, Gladstone, and he was scarcely ever caught out. But to him it was a game in a sense in which it was not to his rivals. Years later in 1877, at the height of the Eastern crisis, he had to remind the Queen that he was not her Grand Vizier. It is hard to believe that he did not regret the fact.

His Turkish experience also shaped his attitude to foreign affairs. Diplomatic crises, as they come up to politicians, are always complicated, confusing, urgent and obscure. But there is very often an instinctive, almost intuitive attitude which conditions the initial approach and which may go far back into the early years of the person concerned. No one who reads Disraeli's own account of his visit to the Near East in 1830–31 could be surprised that he tended to dismiss the Bulgarian atrocities in 1876 as grossly exaggerated and to react with particular distaste against the committees and meetings which took the opposite line in London and all over the country. Of course he studied the papers and the despatches and of course he appreciated that the world was not the same as it had been in 1830–31, but it is unlikely that his views would have been quite what they were if he had never met the Grand Vizier, never seen the Sultan, never smoked a pipe six feet long and never wandered through the Bazaar of Constantinople.

Chapter 4
The Holy City
January–March 1831

I

Disraeli had written on 11 January that he expected to be in Egypt in ten days and return home via Malta and Naples. In fact he was to go first to Smyrna, then to Cyprus, Jaffa and Jerusalem, then back to Jaffa, whence he and Clay sailed for Alexandria which they did not reach till the second week in March 1831. On the face of it, the visit to Jerusalem seems to have been an unpremeditated diversion. Yet this appearance is contradicted by the fact that one of Disraeli's original motives for going on his tour was to get 'copy' for *Alroy* and *Contarini Fleming*. Admittedly the plot of the latter did not require a sight of Jerusalem. Contarini's visit to the city is somewhat dragged in and could easily have been omitted. *Alroy* was a different matter. The hero is a largely mythical Jewish Prince of the twelfth century who has to obtain the sceptre of Solomon from the Tombs of the Kings to lead his followers out of the captivity of a Moslem caliph. No doubt suitable descriptions could be lifted from guide books but a visit to the Holy City would certainly be a help. Precisely what plans were made and changed and remade is not clear, but it is hard to imagine Disraeli readily forgoing this opportunity.

Shortly after 11 January Disraeli and Clay left Constantinople in the *Susan*. Their problem was to get away from Sir Robert Gordon, who even offered them rooms in the 'Palace' to keep them as companions, and 'finally when all was in vain parted from us in a pet'. They had a fair wind down the Dardanelles, but were becalmed for three days between Lesbos and a place described by Disraeli as Zea which is not on modern maps – at least not under that name. 'You cannot conceive anything more lovely than the scenery of the Gulf of Smyrna', he wrote in a long letter to his sister on 20 March 1831 from Alexandria.

> At Smyrna where we intended only to touch for a day, we were detained for ten, by our winter season, violent and unceasing rains and terrible gales of wind. Here, however, we found Meredith in a very decent bivouack, so having much to say to each other got over the affair better than might be expected. This is the only winter we have had, tho' this season at Constantinople is usually even severe. I ascribe to this continuance of fine weather and to smoking the continued improvement in my health, which is most satisfactory.

At Smyrna Disraeli discovered that Meredith, who, it seems, had not intended to rejoin the party, now wanted to see Egypt. One can guess that, especially in regard to the pleasures of Constantinople, Meredith had not seen eye to eye with his two companions, in particular Clay who after several weeks of enforced abstinence would certainly have visited the brothels for which the city was celebrated. According to Disraeli, Meredith had hitherto known 'no more about Egypt than a child', but having picked up in Smyrna W. R. Hamilton's *Aegyptiaca : The Ancient and Modern State* (1810), which contained the earliest translations of the Rosetta Stone, he was 'quite surprised to learn that there were more remains there on one spot than in all the rest of the globe united'. However he resolved to come on later, as 'he could not make up his mind to give up an intended trip to the unseen relics of some unheard of cock and bull city'. So Disraeli and Clay proceeded on their way past Chios through the Sporades towards Rhodes, but, though they were off the island for two days, adverse winds prevented them from landing and they headed for Cyprus where they spent a day 'on a land famous in all ages but more delightful to me as the residence of Fortunatus, than as the rosy realm of Venus or the romantic kingdom of the Crusades'. Fortunatus, the hero of a once popular sixteenth-century fable, was supposed to be a native of Famagusta who stole a magical hat from the Sultan and could thus transport himself wherever he wished.

From Cyprus they sailed with the help of a pilot to Jaffa (which Disraeli invariably spells with one 'f'). There were three main routes to Jerusalem. One was to proceed overland from Acre, St Jean d'Acre, as it was known then, or Akko to modern Israelis; the second was to go from Jaffa and the third was to come up from Egypt via Gaza. Acre had the advantage of being far the best harbour on the coast whereas Jaffa was the worst, but the traveller from Acre or from Egypt had the disadvantage of a land journey at least three times as far at a period when such travel was uncomfortable and hazardous. 'One morning with a clear blue sky and an intense sun we came in sight of the whole coast of Syria, very high and mountainous, and the loftiest ranges covered with snow.' ('Syria' was used in those days of the region of the Ottoman Empire running south from Aleppo and covering modern Syria, Lebanon, Israel and Jordan. 'Palestine', derived from the name of the old Roman province, did not re-emerge into general usage till the establishment of the British Mandate in 1920.) They passed Beirut, Sur (which was the ancient Tyre), and Acre and 'at length cast anchor in the roads of Jafa. Here we made a curious acquaintance in Damiani, the descendant of an old Venetian family but himself a perfect oriental.' He was greatly impressed by their knowledge and if he had not known them to be English would have taken them to be 'Sorcerers'.

> We found him living among the most delightful gardens of oranges, citrons and pomegranates, the trees as high and the fruit as thick as our English apple orchards, himself a most elegant personage in flowing robes of crimson silk . . . He wished us to remain with him for a month, and gave us an admirable Oriental dinner, which would have delighted my father. Rice, spices, pistachio nuts, perfumed rotis, and dazzling confectionery.

They could not linger, however, and were on their way next day to Jerusalem.

From Jafa, a party of six, well mounted and armed, we departed for Jerusalem. Jafa is a pretty town, surrounded by gardens, and situated in a fruitful plain. After riding over this we crossed a range of light hills and came into the plain of Ramle, vast and fertile. Ramle, the ancient Arimathea, is the model of our idea of a beautiful Syrian village, all the houses isolated and each surrounded by palm trees – the meadows, and the exterior of the village covered with olive trees or divided by rich plantations of Indian fig. Here we sought Hospitality in the Latin convent, an immense establishment, well kept up, but with only one monk. I could willingly dwell in immense detail but cannot. The next day we commenced our Journey over the delightful plain, bounded in the distance by the severe and savage mountains of Judea. In the wild stony ravines of these shaggy rocks we were wandering the whole day; at length after crossing a vast hill, we saw the Holy city.

Although Disraeli does not say so, the two-day journey to Jerusalem from Jaffa was regarded by pilgrims and tourists alike as anything but pleasant. The Latin convent to which he refers, the Hospice of St Nicodemus and St Joseph of Arimathea, which was Napoleon's HQ in 1799 and still stands, may have been comfortable enough, but the traveller found the going hard after Ramle. The route which of course was not the same as the modern motor road was in its final stages steep, rocky and exhausting. One had to pay 'protection money' to the Arab Sheikhs who claimed suzerainty over the area, and Disraeli's party was perhaps lucky to go on horseback, for, from time to time, the Porte forbade that mode of transportation to 'infidels', who thus had to ride on donkeys, mules or camels. There was, moreover, a particularly notorious brigand family, the Sheikhs of Abu-Ghosh, whose representative at this time had a force of 200 horsemen and regularly levied an extra tribute from unlucky travellers. The road itself was so bumpy and bestrewn with boulders that no carriage could use it. The first coach made its way from Jaffa to

Jerusalem in 1869, but it conveyed no less a personage than the Emperor Franz-Joseph, and a special effort had been made by the Turkish government to render the road fit for wheeled transport.

The description of the traveller's first view of Jerusalem, which Disraeli gives in his correspondence and repeats almost verbatim in *Contarini Fleming*, is that seen from the Mount of Olives on the east, although Disraeli would not actually have had his first vision of the Holy City from there, for he and his party arrived at the Jaffa or David Gate which is on the west of the Old city. To his sister Disraeli wrote of that extraordinary view from the Mount of Olives – a view which to this day remains one of the wonders of the world :

> This is a very high Hill, still partially covered with the tree which gives it a name. Jerusalem is situated upon an opposite height, which descends as a steep ravine, and forms with the assistance of the mount of Olives, the narrow valley of Jehosaphat. Jerusalem is entirely surrounded by an old feudal wall with towers and gates of the time of the crusaders and in perfect preservation; as the town is built upon a hill, you can from the opposite height discern the roof of almost every house. In the front is the magnificent mosque built upon the site of the Temple, with its beautiful gardens and fantastic gates – a variety of domes and towers rise in all directions, the houses are of a bright stone. I was thunderstruck. I saw before me apparently a gorgeous city. Nothing can be conceived more wild and terrible and barren than the surrounding scenery, dark, stony and severe, but the ground is thrown about in such picturesque undulations, that the mind is full of the sublime, not the beautiful, and rich and waving woods and sparkling cultivation would be misplaced. The city on the other side is in the plain, the ravine not being all round. It is, as it were, in a bowl of mountains. I have dotted down materials for description; I have not space to describe. I leave it to your lively imagination to fill up the rest. Except Athens, I never saw anything more essentially

striking – no city, except that, whose site was so preeminently impressive. I will not place it below the city of Minerva. Athens and Jerusalem in their glory must have been the finest representations of the beautiful and sublime. Jerusalem in its present state, would make a wonderful subject for Martin [John Martin, 1789–1854, historical and landscape painter, famous for his 'Belshazzar's Feast'] and a picture from him could alone give you an idea of it.

The mosque was of course the Dome of the Rock, the Mosque of Omar which, along with the El Aksa close by, constitutes an astonishing spectacle. The golden dome of the one and the silver dome of the other make an impression which is unforgettable. Architecturally they were then, and still are today, the finest buildings in the Old City. Disraeli commented on 'the bright stone' of the houses. This is equally true now, and the words of the famous hymn 'Jerusalem the golden' – unlike those of some hymns – correspond to reality. He was, however, wrong – though not unreasonably so – in thinking that the wall was feudal and dated back to the days of the Latin Kingdom of the Crusaders. It looks like that but was in fact built more than three centuries later in 1538 by the Turkish Sultan Suleiman, the Magnificent, whose father Selim had conquered Syria and Egypt in 1516–17.

There were no houses outside the old walls at this time. The first of the many suburbs which eventually grew into a new city far bigger than the old was built in 1860, thanks to the influence and assistance of Sir Moses Montefiore, one of the greatest of all Jewish philanthropists. At the time of Disraeli's visit the prudent man made a point of not spending the night outside the walls unless well guarded – a consideration which lent added urgency to the exhausting climb on the second day of the journey from Jaffa. There were at this time no inns or hotels in Jerusalem or in the rest of Palestine. The traveller had to seek the hospitality of monasteries, for which of course he paid. Disraeli, Clay and party were guided from the Jaffa Gate to the famous monastery of St Salvador. This was (and is) the headquarters of the Franciscan Order in Jerusalem, also known as *Custodia Terra Santa*, for the Franciscans are the guardians of the Holy Places and the Church of the Holy Sepulchre.

In his letter to Sarah, Disraeli, in order to save a description of his reception at St Salvador, wrote 'for an account of which see Clarke'. The Reverend E.D.Clarke (1769–1822), restless traveller in Europe and the Near East from 1799 to 1802, was an antiquary and mineralogist of eminence. He later became Senior Tutor of Jesus College Cambridge and University Librarian. He began to publish successive volumes giving an account of his travels in 1810 and his description of the Holy Land came out in 1817. His works were widely used as guide books by English travellers. His own visit to Jerusalem had been as long ago as July 1801, but it is unlikely that much had changed in the past thirty years. At any rate Disraeli seems to have found St Salvador as Clarke had found it.

Clarke describes it as 'a large building like a fortress, the gates of which were thrown open to receive our whole cavalcade' and goes on:

> Here being admitted into a court with all our horses and camels, the vast portals were again closed and a party of the most corpulent friars we had ever seen, from the warmest cloisters of Spain and of Italy waddled around us, and warmly welcomed our arrival.
>
> From the court of the Convent we were next conducted by a stone staircase to a refectory where the monks who had received us introduced us to the Superior not a whit less corpulent than his companions.

Clarke contrasted these Franciscans with the Propaganda Missionaries.

> The latter are as meagre and pale as the former are corpulent and ruddy. The life of the missionaries is necessarily a state of constant activity and of privation. The Guardians of the Holy Sepulchre . . . are confined to the walls of their comfortable convent which, when compared with the

usual accommodations of the Holy Land is like a well
furnished and sumptuous hotel, open to all comers whom
curiosity or devotion may bring to this mansion of rest and
refreshment.

Clarke describes the 'refreshment' they received – coffee and 'some
delicious lemonade'. The beds were clean, 'although a few bugs
warned us to spread our hammocks upon the floor where we slept for
once unmolested'. Bedbugs and fleas were the curse of the oriental
traveller in the nineteenth century, and complaints on that score are
echoed in many books. They had an excellent supper in the Pilgrim's
Chamber, and then an Italian in a Francisan habit came in and,
'giving us a wink took some bottles of Noyau from his bosom desiring
us to taste it, he said that he could supply us with any quantity. He
was a confectioner but his principal employment was the manufac-
ture of liqueurs.' Clarke comments : 'Perhaps for sale among the
Moslems who will make any sacrifice to obtain drams of this nature.'

Disraeli makes no mention of this embellishment but it is likely
that in other respects his party were treated on their first night in
much the same way. Thereafter, however, they were given a house
on their own.

> One of the best houses in Jerusalem belonged to the
> convent, and servants were alloted to us. They sent us
> provisions daily. I could write half a dozen sheets on this
> week, the most delightful in all our travels. We dined every
> day on the roof of our house by moonlight – visited the Holy
> Sepulchre of course, tho' avoided the other Coglionerias
> [frauds] ; the house of Loretto is probability to them, but
> the Eastern will believe anything. Surprised at the number of
> remains at Jerusalem – tho' some more ancient than Herod.
> The tombs of the Kings very fine. Weather delicious – mild
> summer heat – made an immense sensation – received visits
> from the Vicar General of the Pope, the Spanish Prior etc.
> Never more delighted in my life.

Disraeli's letter sounds a bit hurried and perfunctory, and, although he declares the week to be the most delightful in his travels, and repeats his delight at the end of the passage just quoted, he described the scenes which he saw in Spain and Yanina much more fully and vividly. But this may have been because he was then still slightly homesick and conscious of faithful promises to write. Prolonged absence does not always make the heart grow fonder. It often makes the memory grow fainter. He was to be away for some sixteen months all told, but only three of the seventeen letters which he wrote to his family during that period were written in its second half. In fact Disraeli was more impressed by and saw more of Jerusalem than his letter conveys. He rightly appreciated, like most men of sense long before his day, that the Church of the Holy Sepulchre was a pious fraud. As he makes Contarini say (Part VI, Chapter VI) :

> Within its walls they have contrived to assemble the scenes of a vast number of incidents in the life of the Saviour, with a highly romantic violation of the unity of place . . . The truth is, the whole is an ingenious imposture of a comparatively recent date, and we are indebted to that favoured individual, the Empress Helen, for this exceedingly clever creation, as well as for the discovery of the true cross.

Contarini described the Church, much of which had been rebuilt after a major fire in 1808, as :

> . . . A spacious building surmounted by a dome. Attached to it are the particular churches of the various Christian sects, and many chapels and sanctuaries. Mass in some part or other is constantly celebrating, and companies of pilgrims may be observed in all directions, visiting the holy places and offering their devotions. Latin and Armenian and Greek friars are everywhere moving about. The court is crowded with the vendors of relics and rosaries. The church of the Sepulchre is itself a point of common union, and in its bustle and lounging character rather reminded me of an exchange than a temple.

This account is not very different from the reality of a century and a half later. What else did Disraeli do during his 'delightful' week? He evidently made the climb to the Mount of Olives, but in his letter to Sarah he does not mention another episode – his attempt to enter the Mosque of Omar, strictly forbidden to infidels, whose dress at once distinguished them. Disraeli wrote some author's notes in an appendix to *Alroy* in the edition of 1845 :

> I endeavoured to enter it at the hazard of my life. I was detected and surrounded by a horde of turbaned fanatics, and escaped with difficulty; but I saw enough to feel that minute inspection would not belie the general character I formed of it from the Mount of Olives. I caught a glorious glimpse of splendid courts and light airy gates of Saracenic triumph, flights of noble steps, long arcades, and interior gardens, where silver fountains spouted their tall streams amid the taller cypresses.

In *Contarini Fleming* the hero speaks of the same experience :

> . . . The Frank [i.e. European] will enter it at the risk of his life. The Turks of Syria have not been contaminated by the heresies of their enlightened Sultan. In Damascus it is impossible to appear in the Frank dress without being pelted : and although they would condescend perhaps, at Jerusalem to permit an infidel dog to walk about in his national dress, he would not escape many a curse and many a scornful exclamation of 'Giaour !' There is only one way to travel in the East with ease, and that is with an appearance of pomp. The Turks are much influenced by the exterior, and although they are not mercenary, a well-dressed and well-attended infidel will command respect.

There is no need to doubt that both Disraeli and Clay fulfilled these requirements admirably.

Disraeli makes no comment in his letter on the political and social condition of Jerusalem. He observes in *Contarini Fleming* : 'As for the interior of Jerusalem it is hilly and clean. The houses are of stone and well built but like all Asiatic mansions they offer nothing to the eye but blank walls and dull portals.' This was not the impression that Jerusalem made on every visitor. There is no reason to think that things had greatly changed eighteen years later when the Reverend J.A.Spencer visited the Holy City in April 1849, apart from the establishment of two inns, at one of which he stayed, Meshullam's Hotel near the Damascus Gate. He arrived in wet weather and wrote :

> To a European or American accustomed to the broad avenues and clean, paved and well-lighted streets of most of our cities and towns, Jerusalem, like all oriental cities must, at first, appear unpleasant and disagreeably dirty. Its streets are very narrow, extremely uneven and by no means free from filth; the nature of the ground on which the city stands, renders it a constant succession of up and down, the street holed in many places, paved in the form of stairs; the evident state of ruin, and almost desolation, which characterises some portions of the town not only annoys the traveller who has to make his way as best he can amid loose stones, dirt and nastiness, but fills his mind with sadness that the Holy City should be thus degraded and brought low.

In a later passage he conceded that once the rain had stopped the streets became relatively dry and clean, that Jerusalem was really no worse than other cities in the near east, and that there was something to be said for high walls and narrow streets after 'one has been exposed to the scorching sun for an hour or so'. Nevertheless 'in general it disappoints the traveller'. No doubt this was true of most Englishmen brought up as they were on the Bible, indeed immersed in its imagery. The Jerusalem of the early nineteenth century bore little resemblance to the rhapsodic vision of the Psalmist. It was a poverty-stricken Turkish city which, however, happened to contain some of the most sacrosanct places hallowed by the three great monotheistic religions of the world. The significance to Jews of the site of the Temple and to Christians of the Church of the Holy Sepulchre is obvious, but the European can too easily forget that Mohammed ascended into heaven from the site of the Dome of the Rock and that Jerusalem, after Mecca and Medina, is the third holiest city of Islam.

Jerusalem was immediately ruled from the Citadel by a Turkish governor but he was a junior figure in a hierarchy. The territory, now known as Palestine to Gentiles, or Erez-Israel (i.e. the Land of Israel) to the Jews, had ceased to be a political or administrative unity since the fall of the Latin Kingdom of the Crusaders. In the early nineteenth century it was divided into two *sanjaks* (or districts). Judaea, Samaria and the northern Negev were governed from Damascus. Galilee and the coastal plain to Gaza were governed from Acre. Both were parts of the *vilayet* (i.e. province) of Beirut. The region, apart from the coastal plain, was impoverished and economically backward – an area of barren mountains and malarial swamps. It had no mineral resources. It was far away from the principal trade routes, such few roads as existed were appalling, and ships called with reluctance at ports which were no better than open roadsteads exposed to every storm. The population, which was overwhelmingly Moslem though it contained small Christian and Jewish minorities, was reckoned, in those non-statistical days, to be somewhere between 150,000 and 300,000. In spite of the Diaspora and the handicaps imposed on them ever since 135 AD, a certain number of Jews had somehow managed to survive. In the early 1800s the number was about 10,000, mostly settled in the so-called 'holy lands' – the towns of Jerusalem, Hebron, Safed and Tiberias, the largest number, 4,000, being in Safed. In 1800 there were some 3,000 Jews in Jerusalem out of a population of about 10,000. In the early 1830s the Jewish population began to increase and by 1840 it was the largest community in the city – 5,000, compared with 4,500 Muslims and 3,500 Christians. In 1860 the Jews were to constitute half of a total population of 20,000. The Jews were town-dwellers not because, as is sometimes alleged, there was something inherently urban about their nature; in fact they are as good, or as bad, as any other religious or racial group at the practice of agriculture. The reason was partly piety and partly security. The rural areas of the Ottoman Empire were even more lawless and under-policed than the towns.

The Turks regarded Christians and Jews with equal contempt. The Christians had the asset of bringing in what would now be called tourist trade in the form of pilgrims, principally Greek Orthodox or Armenian, for the Roman Catholics had ceased to come (hence the availability of St Salvador for non-religious visitors). But their furious quarrels disturbed the peace and they were the excuse for foreign powers advancing their political plans by claiming to 'protect' them. Russia protected the Greeks, and France the few Roman Catholics. In 1840 Britain and Prussia decided to compete by protecting the Protestants, and were in no way deterred by the fact that there were hardly any Protestants to protect, apart from an Evangelical mission engaged in the unrewarding task of converting the Jews.

Jerusalem was divided into areas corresponding to religious beliefs. Not surprisingly the Moslem quarter, adjacent to the Dome of the Rock in the north-east of the city, was the most salubrious place in which to live. 'The Turkish or Mohammedan population', wrote Spencer, 'occupy the north-eastern portion of the city which is the most airy and pleasant. By their position as rulers and in authority, as well as by natural temperament, they are haughty, insolent and tyrannical.' The worst area was the Jewish quarter, where in order to be as insulting as possible the Turks had erected a mosque to offend the spiritual and a slaughter house to offend the physical senses of the Jews. Spencer wrote :

> The Jews occupy the vicinity of Mount Zion or the southern part of the city, and are to a very great extent, a degraded race, depending on charity for support : they are despised and hated by both Mohammedans and Christians: they live in the very narrowest lanes and most filthy and disagreeable quarter of the Holy City ; and they endure scorn and contempt with a hardihood which no other nation or people ever

manifested. Most of them are very poor, and nearly all are supported by contributions from abroad . . . Few persons ever do more than walk or ride through the Jews' quarter, both because it is far from pleasant to make one's way through narrow and dirty streets and because rarely is it possible to penetrate the cold reserve of the degraded Israelite, and be on terms of familiar intercourse as will enable a Christian to appreciate a Jew, or a Jew really to understand a Christian. In general, he has an instinctive dislike to the believer in Christ Jesus ; and, to our shame be it confessed, the dislike and hatred are far too often mutual.

There is nothing to suggest that Disraeli made any contact with the Jews, though he may have ventured into the Jewish quarter. It was one thing for Sir Moses Montefiore who visited Jerusalem four years earlier to make a point of staying in the house of one of the leading rabbis. He was very rich and a strict adherent to the Jewish faith; the whole purpose of his visit was to give what help he could to the Jews of the Holy City. Disraeli in one sense of the word 'Jew', was not a Jew at all. His father had indeed been a somewhat tepid member of the Sephardi synagogue at Bevis Marks, although in reality he was, if anything, an eighteenth-century Deist. After a quarrel with the Presiding Body, the *Mahammad*, he removed his name from the list in March 1817, and that summer, at the insistence of a friend, had his four children baptised by an Anglican clergyman. From the age of twelve Disraeli was a member of the Church of England – a change which had an important effect on his career, for Jews did not become eligible for Parliament until 1858, twenty-one years after he first entered the House of Commons. Of course he was well aware of his Jewish descent and he was keenly interested in the history of 'the race'. But travelling with Clay as a debt-ridden and slightly spurious English 'milord', he would not readily have involved himself in the affairs of the miserable and remote co-religionists of his forebears.

The condition of the Christians in Jerusalem was slightly, but only slightly, better than that of the Jews. The Christian quarter was larger and less over-crowded. It was in practice divided into two – the Armenian and the others. It lay on the west of the city and the Armenian quarter was and is in the south-west. There were at least six varieties of Christianity in more or less continuous conflict: the Greek Orthodox, the Roman Catholic, the Armenian, the Syrian, the Coptic, and the Ethiopian. Greek and Latin Christendom after centuries of uneasy relations had finally divided in 1054, largely on the question of Papal supremacy but also on the doctrine of the 'double procession of the Holy Ghost', in other words whether the Holy Ghost 'proceeded' from the Father alone or from the Son as well (*Filioque*). The Greeks denounced the *Filioque* clause almost as vigorously as they denounced the Pope. The Armenians, Syrians, Copts and Ethiopians had split away from the main line of Christendom at an earlier stage as a result of the Council of Chalcedon in 451. They were Monophysites who held that in the person of the Incarnate Christ there was a single Divine Nature, not, as both Catholics and Orthodox maintained – and still maintain – following the majority at the Council of Chalcedon, a double Nature, Divine and Human.

The bitter and bigoted intra-Christian wrangles about the holy places were a notorious scandal, ill-calculated to convert either Jews or Moslems. They led at times to fisticuffs, woundings, even murder. There was actual bloodshed on occasions in the Church of the Holy Sepulchre itself. The settlement of these disputes went in the end, through a long series of torpid and sceptical authorities, to the Sultan or his ministers. The Porte was influenced partly by power politics, partly by bribery. In terms of power politics, Catholics and Orthodox had the edge on the rest. France and Russia with an eye on the ultimate dissolution of the Ottoman Empire were ready to exploit the ecclesiastical grievances of the creeds they protected, although their efforts often cancelled each other out. Such occasions gave the Armenians, who were adepts at bribery, a chance. They were rich and their wealth compensated for the absence of a protecting power, the Armenian Kingdom having finally disappeared fourteen centuries earlier in 430. Disraeli was well aware of these divisions. *Tancred*, of all his novels, is the one which most depends on his impressions of Jerusalem and 'Syria'. The following dialogue occurs between Tancred and 'the lady' (the beautiful Jewess, Eva) whom Tancred is trying to convert.

'You are already half a Christian !' said Tancred with animation.

'But the Christianity which I draw from your book [the Bible] does not agree with the Christianity which you practise', said the lady, 'and I fear, therefore, it may be heretical.'

'The Christian Church would be your guide.'

'Which ?' enquired the lady. 'There are so many in Jerusalem. There is the good bishop who presented me with this volume and who is himself a Hebrew [see below, p. 78]; there is the Latin Church which is founded by a Hebrew; there is the Armenian Church, which belongs to an Eastern Nation who, like the Hebrews, have lost their country and are scattered in every clime ; there is the Abyssinian Church which hold us in great honour and practise many of our rites and ceremonies ; and there are the Greek, Maronite and the Coptic Churches, who do not favour us but do not treat us as grossly as they treat each other.'

Disraeli in a later passage re-emphasized the parallel between the Armenians and the Jews. Eva says to Tancred:

'Go to Armenia and you will not find an Armenian. They too are an expropriated nation, like the Hebrews. The Persians conquered their land, and drove out the people. The Armenian has a proverb: "In every city of the East I find a home." They are everywhere; the rivals of my people, for they are one of the great races and little degenerated; with all our industry, and much of our energy; I would say with all our human virtues, though it cannot be expected that they should possess our divine qualities; they have not produced

Gods and prophets and are proud that they can trace up their faith to one of the obscurest of the Hebrew apostles [Gregory the Illuminator, 240–332] and who never knew his great master.'

In the dreadful twentieth century this parallel was to be repeated in a way which neither Disraeli nor any of his contemporaries could have predicted. No one is likely to forget the Holocaust, the deliberate murder of six million Jews who fell into German hands in the Second World War. The precedent for this act of genocide is not always remembered, but the fact remains that in June/July 1915 the Turks massacred the vast majority of their Armenian subjects. The exact number will never be known, but according to most authorities it was not less than two million men, women and children, slaughtered in circumstances of the utmost barbarity.

Syria at the time of Disraeli's visit was on the verge of important changes which affected Jerusalem like every other city in the region. In October 1831, soon after Disraeli had returned to England, Mehemet Ali launched what was in effect a rebellion against the Sultan, though in theory it was a war between the Pasha of Egypt and the Pasha of Acre. As in the case of Greece, the Egyptian army was commanded by Mehemet's son, Ibrahim, and once again his forces were victorious. By the beginning of 1833 the Egyptian occupation of Syria was complete. Mehemet Ali introduced a more efficient system of government and enforced law and order to an extent unknown for generations. He also appreciated that the fruits of victory depended to some degree on European acquiescence, for the conquest of Syria potentially menaced the existence of the Sultanate whose disappearance would have a major effect on great-power politics. He, therefore, relaxed at least some of the restrictions on Christian and Jewish pilgrims proceeding to Jerusalem. Taxes and fees were no longer to be collected from them. This enraged not only the Abu Ghosh family but also the local Christians, both ecclesiastical and lay, who had for years past made a useful income from foreign pilgrims. However, it pleased the European powers, and, coupled with the repeal of laws about discriminatory dress and with the representation of Christians – and even Jews – on consultative councils in some towns, it was a step in the direction of toleration. A British vice-consul was installed in Jerusalem in 1838. He had a special charge not only to promote commerce (of which there was anyway very little in Jerusalem) but also to protect the Jews. Christians and Jews were widely employed in the Egyptian administration, and foreign missions, provided they did not try to convert Moslems, were given a freer hand than ever before.

These changes were not reversed after Ibrahim withdrew in 1839 under pressure from the great powers. Many of them were preserved by the Ottomans, who welcomed the restoration of order and the suppression of the more outrageous abuses. They too were anxious to keep in with European opinion and therefore behaved less intolerantly towards non-Moslems. In 1841 after complicated negotiations the British and Prussian governments agreed to create an Anglican See of Jerusalem, the bishop to be nominated alternately by the two crowns. Britain had the first choice. Who better, it was argued, than a converted Jew? And the first bishop was an ex-rabbi from Posen who had become a missionary of the London Society for Promoting Christianity among the Jews, known as the London Jewish Society (LJS) for short. (Hence Eva's remark quoted above about 'the good bishop' being 'a Hebrew'. *Tancred* was published in 1847, well after these events.) His name (originally Wolf) was Michael Solomon Alexander. He was to have been conveyed to Jaffa in a naval frigate called *Infernal*. This was deemed inappropriate both by the bishop and others. Instead he sailed in *Devastation* – an improvement perhaps, if not a great one.

All these changes lay ahead when in March 1831 Disraeli and Clay made their way to the realm of the great Egyptian Pasha, Mehemet Ali himself.

The Turks taking Missolonghi from Greek patriots in 1826. When Disraeli arrived in Greece in 1830 the country had had nine years of particularly fanatical and barbaric warfare.

Athens and the Acropolis, with Turkish soldiers in the foreground.

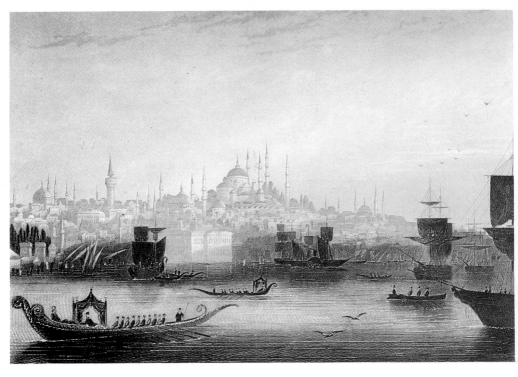

Constantinople. The city produced a feeling of immediate euphoria in Disraeli – 'it baffles all description . . . an immense mass of buildings, cupolas, cypress groves and minarets. I feel an excitement which I thought was dead.'

Sultan Mahmoud II.

The Great Bazaar in Constantinople – 'perhaps a square mile of these arcades intersecting each other in all directions and full of every product of the Empire from diamonds to dates'.

The Mosque of Sultan Ahmet in Constantinople.

An early nineteenth-century view of Jerusalem, with the Mount of Olives out of sight to the left. To his sister, Disraeli wrote: 'I was thunderstruck. I saw before me an apparently gorgeous city.'

Chapter 5

The Land of
Priestcraft and Pyramids
March–October 1831

I

'Here I am at last in the ancient land of Priestcraft and Pyramids,' wrote Disraeli to Sarah from Alexandria in the letter of 20 March quoted in the last chapter. Disraeli and Clay had reached Alexandria from Jaffa a week earlier. They were entertained by the partner of 'Mr. Briggs, the great Egyptian merchant' – in fact Mehemet Ali's sole agent in England. He had written to commend Disraeli as the son of a famous author. As a result they dined every day with the partner, 'whose cuisine is excellent'. In the same letter Disraeli observed: 'It is so long since I have written, altho' I miss no reasonable opportunity of so doing, that I forget what I was about when I wrote to you last.' He then recalled that it was on the eve of leaving Constantinople, 'Meredith having already departed for his exploration of Asia Minor, respecting which he was very mad, altho' I believe it to be a country equally unsatisfactory to the topographer, the antiquarian and the man of taste.' Meredith, however, had been 'bitten' by the notion of Egypt and had decided to rejoin his companions. 'The most surprising news!' wrote Disraeli at the end of the letter. 'Meredith has just arrived as I understand in a Turkish ship – after a horrid passage.' Meredith had written to say that he was threatened with a month's quarantine. 'He will go mad' – and Disraeli undertook to see what could be done through the Consul at Alexandria. He then went on to more important matters. 'I have a most knowing Cypriot servant in the most delicate costume. God bless you all. I am afraid you will never get this, as I am out of the lands of regular posts, ambassadors and public offices.'

Some account of the history of Egypt is needed to explain the state of affairs in 1830. Disraeli once said of Peel that he always traced the steam-engine back to the kettle. There is no need to go back to the Pharaohs or the Ptolemies. It is enough to survey the immediate past. In 1517 Egypt had become an appanage of the Turkish Sultan, Selim, who had at the same time acquired the Caliphate or Imamship (i.e. supreme governance) of the Moslem world from the last of the shadow Caliphs of the line of Hashim in Cairo. But the authority of Constantinople was never complete and the history of the next three centuries was one of intermittent rebellion, subjugation and uncertain suzerainty. Effective power was held by the Mamelukes. This military caste of Circassian origin was organized into bands of five or six hundred mounted warriors commanded by chiefs or Beys. They kept the Fellahin, Turks, Copts and Bedouin who made up the vast majority of the population in a state of terrorized subjection. At the close of the eighteenth century they had reduced the power of the Sultan to a nullity. The Turkish Pasha who represented him in Cairo was a mere figurehead.

Egypt had long been an object of French ambition. As early as 1672, the German philosopher mathematician, Leibniz, a civil servant in the Electorate of Mainz, had advised a general policy for the European states of conquering the non-Christian world rather than fighting each other. His scheme apportioned Egypt to France, and he sent a memorandum to Louis xiv, who seems to have taken it seriously but dropped the idea after he had made up his quarrels with the Sultan. The Duc de Choiseul during the reign of Louis xv drew up a plan for the conquest of Egypt, and his ideas were revived in 1781 by the French ambassador in Constantinople, but it was not till 1798 that a definite decision was made. The Directory, partly as a blow against British commerce and the route to India, partly as a means of getting Bonaparte out of the way, resolved on a military expedition to the Nile. Mameluke oppression of a few French merchants at Alexandria was the excuse, and in July 1798 Bonaparte landed – nominally in order to restore the authority of the Sultan, a pretext which in no way deceived the Sublime Porte.

The extraordinary vicissitudes of the French expedition need not be repeated in detail. Late in July Napoleon destroyed the Mameluke power at the Battle of the Pyramids only to have his own fleet destroyed by Nelson at the Battle of the Nile a few weeks later. In no way disconcerted he resolved early in 1799 to make the traditional move of Egyptian rulers and tried to conquer Syria as a buffer against foreign attack. He captured Jaffa, shooting 2,000 prisoners on the beach, and he reached Acre, but the defence conducted by a British naval officer, Sir Sidney Smith, was too much for him. The French suffered heavy losses and were obliged to retreat to Cairo. After repelling a Turkish invasion at Aboukir in July, Napoleon departed to France in October. The French expeditionary force was now leaderless, and in 1801 it capitulated to British arms. The Mameluke power was to some extent restored, but the Turks were determined to crush it, and, to the wrath of General Hutchinson, (the British commander), murdered a number of the principal Beys in 1802 and made prisoners of the rest. The General forced their release, but in 1803 the British evacuated Alexandria. Meanwhile a new element had been introduced into the combustible politics of Egypt. Among the forces brought in by the Turkish government to cope with their enemies in the Nile delta was an Albanian contingent. The Albanians, who were only surpassed in brutality by Kurdish troops imported slightly later for the same purpose, soon became an *imperium in imperio* and the stage was set for a tripartite battle between the Turks, the Albanians and the Mamelukes – themselves divided into two parties.

One of the Albanian officers was Mehemet Ali, who was born in 1769 in relatively humble circumstances near Kavala, a port on the frontier of Thrace and Macedonia. A junior official and tobacco trader, he enlisted in 1798 and became second-in-command of an Albanian regiment which fought at Aboukir. He was rescued from drowning by one of Sir Sidney Smith's boats. He returned to Egypt in 1801 as commander of his regiment. In 1803 the Albanians in protest against lack of pay broke into revolt. He rapidly rose through a series of battles, conspiracies, intrigues and assassinations. Cairo was in a state of turbulent anarchy until in 1805 the Ulema (the Council of those learned in Islamic tradition) invited him to become Pasha, an appointment confirmed by the Sultan in 1806. In 1807 his armies defeated a British expeditionary force whose captured troops were marched into Cairo along a road lined with stakes impaling the decapitated heads of their fellow soldiers. Four years later, having defeated first the Turks and then the British, he finally settled accounts with the Mameluke Beys who, after being received at the citadel of Cairo with courtesy and coffee, were slaughtered almost to a man on their return journey.

Mehemet Ali continued to acknowledge the suzerainty of the Sultan but he was now *de facto* ruler of Egypt, where he introduced a system of total state socialism – the Pasha of course being himself 'the state'. The result was what one would expect and what one has seen all over the modern world – huge taxation, uneconomic industries, waste of labour, land nationalization, decline in agriculture, rapid inflation and, outside the ruling class, general impoverishment. He spent heavily on the army and the fleet, and, with French advice, modernized them to the point of being the most effective in the Sultan's dominions. By 1819 he had conquered most of Arabia, and in 1820 he started the campaign which led to the subjugation of the Sudan, the foundation of Khartoum and the control of the Red Sea ports. However, he ended anarchy and made the rivers and roads of his empire safer than they had been for many years. If he did not restore law, he at least restored order – of a sort. There are circumstances in which this can be the greatest boon of all.

2

On May 28, over two months after his last letter to the family, Disraeli wrote from Cairo to his sister. He and Clay had been to Thebes and were back to their base.

> My dearest Sa
>
> I have received all your delightful letters March packet inclusive, and one from Ralph, for which give him my warmest thanks. I wrote home to whom I forget [it was in fact to Sarah herself], from Alexandria, about ten weeks ago, giving an account of my Syrian adventures and my visit to Jerusalem, but we are out of the lands of diplomatic bags and I tremble for my despatches. I had intended to write a long letter to my father, giving him a detailed account of my travels in this ancient country, and a miscellaneous sheet to yourself, but the wonderful news which meets me here in a pile of Galignanis has really quite unsettled my mind for such an activity.

The wonderul news to which Disraeli refers concerned the Reform Bill introduced by Lord John Russell in the House of Commons on 1 March, carried on the Second Reading by one vote on 23 March but defeated on an amendment to the motion for going into committee on 20 April. Amidst scenes of wild excitement, William IV two days later personally appeared in the House of Lords to dissolve parliament. The result of the elections was a decisive Whig majority. Disraeli's back numbers of Galignani only brought him as far as the news of the majority of one. He rightly guessed that the Bill could hardly survive. This was no reason for worry, as far as he was concerned. A general election on the old franchise was inevitable and certain to produce a majority for reform. A second election after the Bill had been passed would give him his chance to stand. He was anxious now to get home as soon as he reasonably could. 'I am only waiting here for a ship to convey me to Malta, and in all probability shall come home straight.' He would give her 'only a rapid sketch of my progress, which must be finished and colored when we meet'.

Disraeli reassured her about Meredith, for evidently the family was in some way uneasy over their parting – perhaps fear of the bad influence of Clay.

> I am glad that you are not as astonished as the rest at Meredith and myself parting. Considering that Egypt and Syria formed two prominent objects of my travels, and that he had so positively arranged that certainly the last and, in all probability the second [*sc.* first] would not suit him I am surprised, I confess, at their marvelling. Had it not been for the affairs of the yacht which held out to me the advantage of reaching Syria, which otherwise I should not have been able to accomplish, we must have originally parted at Malta.

This passage is slightly obscure but it would seem that Disraeli had originally intended to go straight from Malta to Egypt, perhaps hoping to get himself from there to Jerusalem overland, whereas Meredith meant to go to Constantinople. Clay's yacht had made it possible to combine these plans up to a point. Disraeli went on to say that 'Meredith – who by the bye is looking excessively well – is now at Thebes', the celebrated ruins near Luxor, but would soon return. It would be three or four weeks before Disraeli could sail from Alexandria, and so they would probably leave together. Even if not, they would certainly meet at Malta, as Disraeli would have to pass his quarantine there. 'This is a very inelegant epistle but I am writing it at night, with at least fifty mosquitos buzzing about and biting me in all directions, which destroys sentences.'

One problem of his life in Cairo was that James Clay was ill.

Clay has got an intermittent fever, which in itself is bad
enough, and as he has never been ill before in his life, he is
exceedingly frightened. Luckily here is a very good Frank
physician. I rather imagine he will go off in a day or two to
Rosetta for change of air. I am very well indeed and find the
climate of Egypt delicious – very hot, but always a most
refreshing breeze. I am very sorry about my companion, as
he has been to me a highly agreeable one. I owe much to his
constant attentions. It is a great thing to travel with a man
for months and that he should never occasion you an uneasy
moment, which I can sincerely say of him. Indeed I am
greatly indebted to him for much comfort. You know that
tho' I like to be at my ease, I want energy in those little affairs
of which life greatly consists. Here I found Clay always ready
– in short he saved me from much bore.

We happen to have Clay's version of this relationship too. Disraeli,
he told Meredith, was a person 'who ought never to travel without a
nurse'. Clay was not the only member of the party to be ill. 'Tita',
despite his robust constitution and appearance of abounding health,
was afflicted with dysentery in an acute form.

Thus you see the strong men have all fallen while I who
am an habitual invalid am firm on my legs, but the reason is
this, that I, being somewhat indolent and feeble, live *à la
Turque* while Clay and Giovanni are always in action and
have done nothing but shoot and swim from morning to
night. As I am on the chapter of domestic troubles, you will
hear with regret that my favourite servant, a Greek of
Cyprus, gave me warning yesterday, his father being very ill
at Alexandria. He leaves me directly which is a great bore at
this moment especially as I am about to be alone, and would
annoy me at all times, because he wore a Mameluke dress of
crimson and gold with a white turban thirty yards long, and
a sabre glittering like a rainbow. I must now content myself

with an Arab attendant in a blue shirt and slipperless. How are the mighty fallen!

He congratulated Sarah on her letters, 'in every respect charming – very lively and witty, and full exactly of the stuff I want'. But he was mildly critical of her punctuation – a case of pot and kettle if ever there was. He went on:

> Thank my mother for her remembrance of me. I cannot write to say I am quite well, because the enemy still holds out, but I am sanguine, very, and am at any rate quite well eno' to wish to be home. I shall enquire about Nairoli[1], but for perfumes I rather think Stamboul was the best place. Mustapha's shop there, the Imperial perfumer, was my daily lounge and I never went to the Bazaar without smoking a pipe with him. I don't think I ever mentioned this character to you – remember when we meet. He never showed me Naroli however, tho' he did everything to tempt me to daily expense. The great perfume among the Turks is Atar of Jasmine. I have some – which I sent to Malta with all my goods, some of which will ornament Bradenham in the shape of pipes nine feet long, and curious Oriental arms. I never bought anything, but with a view to its character as furniture. Everything is for Bradenham.

He talked affectionately of his father and was delighted with his 'capital progress'. 'How I long to be with him, dearest of men.' He envisaged them both writing together with vigour and energy, 'which we will do, now that I have got the use of my brain for the first time in my life'. He commented on the family's efforts to obtain a commission in the army for James. 'Jem's commission would occasion me much anxiety, if I did not know that anxiety was useless . . . Tell James I am highly pleased with him and have no doubt he will turn out to be an honour to the family, and that I

---

[1] Sarah had asked about this oil, which was a basis for various perfumes and was extracted from orange blossom.

shall always be his friend.' Nor did he neglect the elder of his two brothers.

> Tell Ralph to write as often, and as much as he likes, and that I have become a most accomplished smoker, carrying that luxurious art to a pitch of refinement of which he has no idea. My pipe is cooled in a wet silken bag, my coffee is boiled with spices, and I finish my last chibouque with a sherbet of pomegranate. Oh! the delicious fruits that we have here and in Syria – orange gardens miles in extent, citrons, limes, pomegranates – but the most delicious thing in the world is a Banana, which is richer than a Pineapple. How I long for my dear father, and how he would wash his mouth in a country where the principal art of life is to make a refreshing drink.

And there was sad news to acknowledge, the death of the family's Newfoundland puppy. Sarah sent him Isaac's epitaph on this amiable creature:

> Max, true descendant of Newfoundland race,
> Where once he sported, finds his burial place.
> Few were his months, yet huge of form tho' bland,
> Well tutored by our James with voice and hand.
> Mild in his pensive face his large dark eyes
> Talked in their silence to our sympathies.
> His awful paw our fond salute would hail,
> And pleasure fluttered in the o'ershadowing tail.
> Vast limb'd, his step resounding as he walk'd,
> The playful puppy like a lion stalk'd;
> All clad in spotless snow he seemed to stand
> Like faultless marble from the sculptor's hand.
> Domestic friend, companion of all hours!
> Our vacant terraces and silent bow'rs
> No more repeat thy name, and by this urn
> Not to love dogs too well we sadly learn.

Disraeli wrote: 'The death of Max has cut me to the heart. The

epitaph is charming and worthy of the better days of our poetry . . .
It is like an inscription by Sophocles translated by Pope.'

He then gave Sarah a résumé of his activities in Egypt since he
last wrote in March:

> I have gossipped a great deal with you. It is impossible to
> say when I will be home but I should think in three months. I
> do not look upon Quarantine as a bore except that it keeps
> me from you. I want rest. From Alexandria from whence I
> wrote to you last, I crossed the desert to Rosetta. It was a
> twelve hours job, and the whole way we were surrounded by
> a mirage of the most complete kind. I was perpetually
> deceived, and always thought I was going to ride into the
> sea. At Rosetta I first saw the mighty Nile, with its banks
> richly covered with palm groves. A grove of palms is the most
> elegant thing in Nature. From Rosetta five days in a capital
> boat, which the Consul had provided for us with cabins and
> every convenience and which recently he had had entirely
> painted and fitted up for Lord Clare, took us to Cairo
> through the famous Delta. This greatly reminded me of the
> rich plains of the Pays Bas – quite flat with a soil in every part
> like the finest garden mould – covered with production but
> more productive than cultivated. The banks of the river
> studded with villages of mud, but all clustered in palm
> groves beautiful – moonlight on the Nile indescribably
> charming and the palms by this light perfectly magical.

He and Clay thus arrived at what Disraeli calls 'Grand Cairo'. It was
'a large town of dingy houses of unbaked brick, looking terribly
dilapidated, but swarming with population in rich and varied
costume'. After a long history of siege, revolution, *coups d'état*,
treachery and massacre, the city was for the moment reasonably
peaceful. They went out to see the Pyramids and ascended the Great
Pyramid, from which only a few weeks later a man whom Disraeli
had briefly met in Spain was to fall to his death – probably suicide.
Disraeli and Clay then went by the same boat up the Nile in a

three-week voyage to Dendera and Thebes. Meredith was no doubt still in quarantine. For whatever reason he made his visit to Thebes later and on his own. Disraeli observed that the river banks were very different from the Delta.

> The land is however equally rich, the soil being formed by the Nile, but on each side at the distance of 3 or 4 miles, and sometimes much nearer, Deserts. The Lybian Desert on the African side is exactly our common idea of a desert, an interminable waste of burning sand, but the Arabian and Syrian deserts very different; in fact what we call Downs. Landing on the African side one night, where the Desert stretches to the very banks, found a ship of Hadgees [pilgrims] emptied on the shore in the most picturesque groups, some squatting down with their pipes, some boiling coffee, some performing their devotions.

After watching the pilgrims for a while Disraeli strolled for nearly a mile away from the bank of the Nile. The weather was close and stifling, although it had been fine and clear for most of the day. Suddenly the sky darkened, and Disraeli was alarmed to see a column of sand rapidly approaching.

> It struck me directly what it was. I rushed to the boat with full speed – but barely quick enough. I cannot describe the scene of horror and confusion. It was a Simoom. The wind was the most awful sound I ever heard. Five columns of sand taller than the Monument emptied themselves on our party. Every sail was rent to pieces, men buried in the earth. Three boats sailing along overturned, the crews swam to shore – the wind, the screaming, the shouting, the driving of the sand were enough to make you mad. We shut all the windows of the cabin, and jumped into bed, but the sand came in like fire. I do not offer this as a description, but as a memorandum for further details.

Disraeli was greatly struck by his journey up the Nile. The antiquities and ruins of that extraordinary civilization were unforgettable.

As for Dendera and Thebes and the remains in every part of upper Egypt, it is useless to attempt to write. Italy and Greece mere toys to them, and Martin's [see p.66] inventions common place. Conceive a feverish and tumultuous dream full of triumphal gates, processions of paintings, interminable walls of heroic sculpture, granite colossi of Gods and Kings, prodigious obelisks, avenues of Sphynxs and halls of a thousand columns, thirty feet in girth and of a proportionate height. My eyes and mind yet ache with grandeur so little in union with our own littleness – there the landscape too was quite characteristic, mountains of burning sand, vegetation unnaturally vivid, groves of cocoa trees, groups of crocodiles and an ebony population in a state of nudity armed with spears of reeds.

Having followed the course of the Nile for seven hundred miles to the very confines of Nubia, we returned. As an antiquary I might have been tempted to advance to have witnessed further specimens, but I was satisfied, and I wished not to lose time unnecessarily. We were a week at Thebes with the advantage of the society of Mr. Wilkinson [Sir John Wilkinson, 1797–1875, the celebrated explorer and Egyptologist], an Englishman of vast learning, who has devoted ten years to the study of hieroglyphics and Egyptian antiquity, and who can read you the side of an obelisk, or the front of a pylon, as we would the last number of the Quarterly.

The exact timing of Disraeli's voyage and return is not quite clear, but if he is right in saying that it took three weeks to reach Thebes and that they stayed there for a week, one can allow seven weeks for the expedition, which may well have occupied April and a large part of May. Having returned to Cairo he took things easily, keeping an eye on Clay who was again ill. 'This Cairo in spite of its dinginess is a luxurious and pleasant place. The more I see of Oriental life the more I like. There is much more enjoyment than at Constantinople.' One curious experience came his way – an encounter with Mehemet Ali.

> I have seen the Pacha [sic] in a very extraordinary manner. Wandering in the gardens of his palace at Shubra, I suddenly came upon him one afternoon surrounded by his Court, a very brilliant circle, in most gorgeous dresses, particularly the black eunuchs in scarlet and gold, and who ride white horses. I was about to retire, but one of his principal attendants took me by the arm and led me to the circle. The Pacha is exceedingly fond of the English. His Highness was playing chess with his fool, and I witnessed a very curious scene. I stayed about a quarter of an hour, and had I waited till his game was finished, I am informed that he would have spoken to me, but as I had no interpreter with me, and am pretty sure that he was in the same state, I thought it best to make my bow. My presentation has been delayed on account of Clay's illness, but it has been offered to me several times. I look forward to it rather as a bore than not – as he receives you quite alone and cross-examines you to a death.

Disraeli was in the end presented to the Pasha, and, whatever actually happened, he later gave an entertaining account of the interview. It appears in a political tract which he published four years later in December 1835 with the somewhat orotund title of *Vindication of the English Constitution in a Letter to a Noble and Learned Lord*, the author being described as 'Disraeli the Younger'. The Learned Lord was Lord Lyndhurst, who had twice been Tory Lord Chancellor and to whom Disraeli was acting as an informal political private secretary. There is some evidence to suggest that they shared the same mistress at that time in the person of Henrietta Sykes (though it is by no means clear that Disraeli accepted the situation –he may have had no choice). The *Vindication* was a defence of the

House of Lords and in the course of it Disraeli casts doubt on the
accepted liberal view of parliamentary representation.

> The current of these observations reminds me of an anec-
> dote which may perhaps amuse your lordship nor be found
> altogether devoid of instruction. When I was in Egypt, the
> pacha of that country, a personage, as is well known, of rare
> capacity, and influenced by an almost morbid desire of
> achieving in an instant the great and gradual results of
> European civilisation, was extremely desirous, among other
> objects of passion or of fancy, of obtaining a Parliament . . .
> It so happened that a young English gentleman, who was on
> his travels, was at this period resident in Cairo, and as he had
> more than once had the good fortune of engaging the atten-
> tion of the pacha by the readiness or patience of his replies,
> his Highness determined to do the young Englishman the
> honour of consulting him.

The young Englishman was of course Disraeli himself, who never
suffered from undue modesty. He describes how he went to the
citadel.

> He found the pacha surrounded by his courtiers, his en-
> gineers, his colonels and his eunuchs. At length his Highness
> clapped his hands and the chamber was cleared, with the
> exception of a favourite minister and a faithful dragoman.
> The surprise of our countryman, when he received the
> communication of the pacha, was not inconsiderable; but he
> was one of those, who had been sufficient of the world never
> to be astonished, not altogether untinctured with political
> knowledge, and gifted with that philosophical exemption
> from prejudice, which is one of the most certain and the most
> valuable results of extensive travel. Our countryman com-
> municated to the Egyptian ruler with calmness and with
> precision the immediate difficulties that occurred to him and
> explained to the successor of the Pharaohs and the Ptolemies
> that the political institutions of England had been the gra-

dual growth of ages, and that there is no political function which demands a finer discipline or a more regulated preparation, than the exercise of popular suffrage.

Mehemet Ali listened in silence, occasionally nodding his head in approval, 'then calling for coffee, instead of looking at his watch like an European sovereign, delicately terminated the interview'. Soon afterwards 'the young Englishman' attended, as he was wont to do from time to time, the Pasha's *levée*. He was beckoned to the contiguous divan.

'God is great!' said Mehemet Ali to the traveller; 'you are a wise man – Allah! Kerim, but you spit pearls. Nevertheless I will have a parliament, and I will have as many parliaments as the King of England himself. See here!' So saying, his Highness produced two lists of names, containing those of the most wealthy and influential personages of every town and district in his dominions. 'See here!' said he, 'here are my parliaments; but I have made up my mind, to prevent inconvenience, to elect them myself.'

Disraeli considered this to be an excellent arrangement. No doubt he is writing to some extent tongue-in-cheek, but not entirely.

Behold, my Lord, a splendid instance of representation without election! In pursuance of the resolution of Mehemet Ali, two chambers met at Cairo: called, in the jargon of the Levant, the *alto Parliamento* and the *basso Parliamento*. The first consisted of the pachas and chief officers of the capital: the second really of the most respectable of the provincial population. Who can doubt that the *basso Parliamento* of Cairo if the invasion of Syria had not diverted the attention of Mehemet Ali from domestic politics, might have proved a very faithful and efficient national council. . . ? Who can hesitate in believing that there was a much greater chance of its efficiency and duration when appointed by the pacha himself, than when elected by his subjects in their present condition?

Disraeli considered that such a parliament had far more chance of survival than the shallow-rooted legislative assemblies recently emerging in Naples or Madrid.

> . . . especially as, it is but candid to confess, Mehemet Ali had further secured a practical term of political initiation for his future legislators by two capital rules; first that the *basso Parliamento* should only petition and not debate; and secondly that the *alto Parliamento* should only debate and not vote!

It is not easy to know how seriously one should take this anecdote. It is not in his contemporary correspondence, but this proves nothing. His last letter from Egypt was dated 28 May, though he stayed on in Cairo for another two months, and the episode might well have occurred then. There is probably at least some core of truth, in the sense that Disraeli is unlikely to have invented it altogether. But the actual details and dialogue may well have been embellished in retrospect. Disraeli could never resist a good story.

3

Disraeli and Clay stayed on in Cairo waiting for Meredith, who had gone to Thebes after them and on his own, and did not get back till the end of June. It must have been at about this time that Disraeli became acquainted with one Paul Emile Botta, who made a great impression on him. In September 1833 Disraeli began what is sometimes called the 'Mutilated Diary', so described because he, or someone else, tore a good many pages out of it later. It is not a diary in any ordinary sense of the word – rather, a series of disconnected and not always intelligible jottings. In an early and reasonably coherent passage he wrote:

> All men of high imagination are *indolent*. I have not gained much in conversation with men. Bulwer is one of the few with whom my intellect comes into collision with benefit. He is full of thought, and views at once original and just . . . But the man from whom I have gained most in conversation is Botta, the son of the Italian historian, whom I knew in Egypt, travelling as a physician in the Syrian dress – the most philosophical mind that I ever came in contact with. Hour after hour has glided, while, *chibouque* in mouth, we have disserted together on our divan, in a country where there are no journals and no books. My mind made a jump in these high discourses. Botta was wont to say that they formed also an era in his own intellectual life. If I add to these my father, the list comprises the few men from whose conversation I have gained wisdom.

Botta, born in 1805, has an important place in the history of archaeology. He became French Consul in Mosul in 1842 and shares much of the credit, along with Sir Henry Layard, Benjamin Austen's nephew, for the great Assyrian excavations of those times, in particular at the famous palace-city of Khorsabad. Later a portrait of him was placed in the Assyrian department of the Louvre. He was moved to Jerusalem, partly for political reasons arising from the revolution of 1848. A small street running off the King David Road is named after him. He later became Consul in Tripoli, where he died in 1872. No evidence of the nature of his 'high discourses' with Disraeli has survived. There are one or two letters in Disraeli's papers written after they had parted. The tone is not exactly 'high'. In July 1832 he wrote from Jamnia (near modern Yahve in Israel), 'As for the women for we must always come to that, some of them are beautiful ... but above all they have an artificial quality which pour un homme blasé gives them all the charms of novelty.' Preceding his next paragraph with the words 'Don't blush. I shall be as chaste as possible', he then gives an interesting but unprintable account of the Arab technique of ensuring the virginity of their women before marriage and securing the maximum of pleasure afterwards. 'What do you think of that? Is it not worth coming to Jamnia?' He went on, in slightly incoherent English, with gaps that have to be conjectured:

> Now my dear Sir I must leave that subject though a very funny one. By this time you have breathed the air of England and I do not know what effect it may have produced upon you. If I have been beyond the rules I pray you pardon me and remember that [if we] have so many tedious books of travels it is because the travellers [never] say things as they are but keep concealed the very things which ought to be known if we want to have at least a true description of the species.
>
> This letter is long enough and I must put an end to it. But before, I will thank you again as well as Mr. Clay for the works of L. Byron. They are my only moral enjoyment and I can say my only society.

In another letter he dwells on the pleasures of smoking opium – to which he later introduced Layard, who luckily became too sick to go on with it. On 30 April 1834 he again wrote to Disraeli:

> Vous pouvez m'addresser vos lettres chez mon pere. Permettez moi d'esperer que quoique wine soit still exciting and Women still beautiful vous trouverey un moment a perdre en ma faveur.
>
> Je ne vous ecris pas en Anglais car j'ai presqu' oublié le peu que j'en savais.
>
> Rappelay moi au souvenir de Mr. Clay. S'est il enfin debarrasse de sa noble lady?

Botta did not further impinge on Disraeli's life. It would still be interesting to know something about their 'high discourses' and just what Disraeli learned from them, but the chance of doing so now is remote.

A terrible disaster then occurred. Meredith arrived back from Thebes, as expected, late in June. The travellers made plans for a leisurely return to England. Clay had gone ahead to Alexandria to organize the voyage, leaving the others to follow him from Cairo, when Meredith was struck down by smallpox and died on July 19. The disease was not diagnosed as being in its most lethal form and the patient seemed to be making good progress. The doctor who had ministered earlier to Clay assured Disraeli, so he told his father in an agonized letter written the day after Meredith's death, 'that all would go well, that it was of a kind that was never fatal, that it must take its course, that he would not even be marked'. Meredith felt no pain and no fear.

> About 5 o'clock one of his attendants came running into the room where I was conversing with a son of Botta, the historian, a very scientific traveller and a surgeon, and told me that his master had fainted. I took Botta along with me, who opened a vein – the blood flew but not strongly, the body was quite warm. The terrible truth apparent to all never occurred to me. But I will not dwell on my own horrible

sufferings, and so much now depends on me that I feel I must exert myself. I would willingly have given up my life for his . . . Our innocent lamb, our angel is stricken. Save her, save her. I will come home directly . . . My dear father I do not know whether I have done all that is necessary. It requires great exertion not to go distracted. I have sent a courier to Clay. Mr. Botta has been very kind to me as I could not sleep and dared not be alone and my anguish was overwhelming.

It was a tragic ending to the Grand Tour – an unpredictable disaster, which afflicted his sister more than anyone but also deeply distressed Disraeli and the whole family. The travellers had intended to go back via Malta, Naples, Rome and Venice, and thence overland to Calais. Disraeli now decided to return as quickly as he could. After a month of infinitely tedious quarantine in Malta he took the first boat to England, arriving late in October. Clay stuck to the original plan. Hence his letter, quoted earlier, from the Lazaretto in Venice (see pp. 20–21).

On the voyage home Disraeli made a friendship which by a curious turn of events was to do him much harm in the eyes of a political figure of great importance in his career. His companion was Henry Stanley, younger brother of Edward Stanley, Whig Secretary for Ireland and later, as 14th Earl of Derby, three times Conservative Prime Minister. Disraeli could not have guessed how closely his own political fortunes were to be entwined with those of the House of Stanley, one of the oldest, richest and grandest in England. The two young men landed at Falmouth and took the coach to London, stopping at Exeter because Disraeli had been hit by some kind of illness. They duly arrived in London and parted; Disraeli to stay for a night or so at the Union Hotel; Stanley ostensibly to return home. However, he did not appear there and his family were soon extremely worried. Sir Philip Rose, examining a number of letters which no longer survive in the Disraeli papers, wrote:

> Steps were taken to trace him. He was at length run to
> earth at Effie Bond's the keeper of the Hell in St. James's

Street where he had taken up his quarters and to which it was alleged Disraeli had introduced him. It would appear from the letters that they had been there together, and as Disraeli was known to have money relations with the Bonds the rest was assumed. The letters from Lord Stanley, his father, and Colonel Long, his brother-in-law, conclusively show that *they* had no complaint against Disraeli; and not only acquitted him of all blame, but were grateful for his interference and aid, and the Hon. Henry's own letters show that Disraeli had given him the best and most disinterested advice.

Unfortunately the member of the Stanley family who really mattered, Henry's elder brother, refused to accept this view. He believed that Disraeli, while apparently working day and night to discover Henry's whereabouts, was all the while party to a conspiracy to inveigle him even further into the clutches of the Bond brothers. Edward Stanley's interpretation of these events did Disraeli much harm, though it was very unfair. There is no reason to doubt that the letters seen by Sir Philip Rose, but now missing, would have confirmed his version of their contents. Disraeli had many failings, but dishonourable conduct of that sort was not one of them. Rose wrote:

> Lord Derby [i.e. Edward Stanley] conceived a strong prejudice against Disraeli, and it was not until the force of public and political affairs forced them to become associates that his hostility disappeared. It is probable that his feeling was rather the resentment of a proud man at a stranger having become mixed up in his family secrets, and cognizance of a brother's misconduct, than any real distrust or belief that his brother had been led into difficulties by Disraeli.

Disraeli did not become aware of this hostility till much later, and the repercussions lie outside the scope of this narrative. His efforts to discover his missing friend delayed his return to Bradenham, perhaps not altogether against his will, for the meeting with Sarah was bound to be painful. He was, however, at Bradenham by the end of November and stayed there for a couple of months before taking lodgings in London, and there we can leave him, 'pretty well,' as he told Austen on January 6, 'having just left off a six weeks' course of Mercury which has pulled me down, but head all right and working like a tiger.'

Chapter 6

The Aftermath

I

It is not easy to quantify the influence of a particular experience on a man's life. Obviously Disraeli's sixteen months in the Near East had some effect upon his career, but one should not exaggerate it. The main steps, his entry into Parliament, his part in the overthrow of Peel, his ascent in society and politics to the top of what he called 'the greasy pole' when at last he became Prime Minister, would no doubt have occurred whether or not he had gone on his Grand Tour. But his thought, writings, outlook and personality, perhaps even his views on foreign policy, might well have been different if he had never set out on his travels. In any case the experience marked him out from the ordinary run of young men. It was not too difficult for a determined traveller to visit all the places that he and his companions saw, but not many people did so in practice, and fewer still spent such a long time there. The older dangers of piracy and brigandage, though still existent, were not as acute as they had been, but the Near East had a well-deserved reputation for being unhealthy. Jerusalem, Jaffa and Cairo had suffered from plague within recent years. Cholera was endemic, and smallpox, product of overcrowded, insanitary, urban conditions, was a serious threat. It carried off Meredith in the prime of life. Malaria, too, was rife, and, in its most acute form, it could be lethal. Clay suffered from 'intermittent fever' which may have been a form of it. Disraeli seems to have been remarkably fit throughout. Whether it was because of the sunshine which he loved or his decision to live lazily *à la Turque* or some other reason, his health was excellent, apart from the malady for which mercury was prescribed – presumably some form of venereal disease which, however, did him, as far as is known, no lasting harm.

As for the psychological illness which had afflicted him since 1826 and which it was one of the objects of his tour to cure, it seems to have vanished. His lengthy sojourn in foreign parts, in some way which cannot easily be explained, brought this phase of his life to an end. In that respect the tour was a complete success, and Disraeli was never again to be a prey to the despondency and despair which he proclaimed in his early home letters, although in the 1830s he was to go through experiences every bit as exhausting and nerve-racking as those which followed the 'hour of adventure' when in 1824 he launched himself so recklessly into the excitements of speculation. Disraeli was now fit to face the hazards of the social and political ascent on which he was determined. He needed to be, for it was a perilous climb made the more so by his own foibles, eccentricities and extravagancies.

There can be no doubt that of all his many experiences on his tour the one that left the greatest and most lasting impression upon him was the visit to Jerusalem. One would not necessarily think so from his contemporary letters, which are longer and more vivid about Spain, Malta, Albania and Egypt, but it was the Holy Land to which he recurrs again and again later, both in his novels and elsewhere. It is not fanciful to see in his few days there the origins of his intense interest in what he called 'the race' – an interest which had been lacking hitherto in the rather indifferent atmosphere of his upbringing. Jerusalem fascinated him because of its scenes and sights, its biblical associations and its dramatic sectarian conflicts. He was intrigued by the great mosques and the imperious power of Islam. He saw the Wailing Wall and he was sympathetically aware of the depressed and poverty-stricken condition of the mass of the Jewish community, even if he had no direct dealings with them during his brief stay. But the phenomenon which interested him most, because of personal parallels however far-fetched, was the part played less in Jerusalem than in 'Syria' as a whole by the successful Jews, those who mysteriously rose up in this alien world through its interstices and became rich and powerful and grand – the Rothschild equivalents in the Near East.

The opportunity to rise in this way stemmed from the double standards of the Turkish system. The pashas or provincial governors, usually in office only for brief periods, had to make their fortunes, like their Roman analogues of old, as quickly as possible and they had also to keep some form of accounts. In theory they were bound by Islamic law with its tiresome restrictions on usury and other modern financial techniques. In practice the pasha needed an adviser who would ignore these rules. Educated Muslims were liable to take them seriously and in any case preferred judicial to administrative employment. No pasha wanted the equivalent of the Ayatollah Khomeini breathing down his neck. Infidels were safer. They were not bound by Islamic law, and as unprotected servants of Muslim masters they dared not question the orders they received. At the pasha's whim they might lose their fortunes, even their lives. From the point of view of Islam Christians and Jews were equally contemptible, but in the early nineteenth century the Christians began to be regarded as more dangerous – a potential fifth column for the European powers which had an eye on the disruption of the Ottoman Empire. The Jews had no such foreign base, and they consolidated their position by an ingenious device. They kept their accounts in Hebrew, written in a calligraphy so obscure as to be barely decipherable. It was as if a Scottish-based firm of London accountants preserved their clients' records in Gaelic written backwards. It was more trouble than it was worth to get rid of such advisers, and one or two Jewish families even established a quasi-hereditary status which led them to wealth and influence. It was no doubt Jews such as these whom Disraeli had in mind when he invented the character, Adam Besso, in *Tancred* to whom the hero is given a letter of credit in Jerusalem by Sidonia, Disraeli's version of Baron Lionel de Rothschild:

MY GOOD ADAM – If the youth who bears this require advances, let him have as much gold as would make the right-hand lion on the first step of the throne of Solomon the King; and if he want more, let him have as much as would form the lion that is on the left; and so on through every stair of the royal seat. For all which will be responsible to you the child of Israel, who among the Gentiles is called SIDONIA.

It may perhaps be doubted whether any Rothschild ever couched a letter of credit quite in these words but Disraeli can be forgiven for using the licence of the novelist.

2

The novels which most vividly display the influence on Disraeli of the Grand Tour and particularly Syria are: *Contarini Fleming*, published by Murray in 1832; *The Wondrous Tale of Alroy*, published along with *The Rise of Iskander* in March 1833 by Saunders and Otley (Murray having returned the MS unread); and *Tancred*, which appeared many years later in March 1847 under the imprint of Colburn, who had become Disraeli's regular publisher from the mid-1830s onwards. Disraeli wrote in his diary that in *Vivian Grey*, 'I have portrayed my active and real ambition. In *Alroy* my ideal ambition.' *Contarini* he described as 'a developmt of my poetic character,' and he added, 'This Trilogy is the secret history of my feelings. I shall write no more about myself.'

Of these *Contarini Fleming* – which was sub-titled 'an Auto-biographical Romance', though Disraeli regarded it as his best novel and though it undoubtedly has considerable biographical interest – is the least important from the point of view of the Grand Tour. Part V is a sort of travelogue in which the hero visits in fiction the same places as Disraeli did in reality. As has already been noticed, great chunks of the *Home Letters* are produced verbatim in these chapters. It is clear that Disraeli was writing parts of this book while he was on his travels. In the preface to the 1845 edition of *Contarini* he refers to it as having been 'written with great care, after deep meditation, and in a beautiful and distant land favourable to composition, with nothing in it to attract the passions of the hour'. Perhaps the letters were copied from the chapters, not vice versa as is usually assumed. It is clear that he also wrote much of *Alroy* before his return to England, although *Iskander*, the short story which was published with it, was written during a visit to Bath in the company of Bulwer-Lytton during the winter of 1832–3.

Iskander is only of interest as showing the use Disraeli made of his Albanian visit. Just as *Alroy* is an account of a twelfth-century Jewish Prince's rebellion against Islamic power, so *Iskander* is a somewhat similar though much shorter *conte*, based on a fifteenth-century Albanian Christian prince who challenged the power of the Sultan Murad II, though in this case it was a successful challenge and did something to delay the fall of Constantinople till 1453. His Turkish name was Skanderbeg and Disraeli must have been familiar with Gibbon's account of this circumcised, Muslim-educated scion of a Christian father who served and then double-crossed the Sultan. He was supposed by his admirers to have been a secret Christian all along. Gibbon observes:

> But he had imbibed from his ninth year the doctrines of the Koran; he was ignorant of the Gospel; the religion of a soldier is determined by authority and habit; nor is it easy to conceive what new illumination at the age of forty could be poured into his soul. His motives would be less exposed to the suspicion of interest or revenge, had he broken the chain from the moment that he was sensible of its weight.

Disraeli's fictionalized version is naturally rather different, but *Iskander* throws no great light on him except in his capacity as an observer and a tourist.

Alroy is a very different affair. It has been rightly condemned for its extravagancies, for its stilted poetical prose, for the absurdity of the plot, and – though less reasonably – for its lack of correspondence with anything that we know about David Alroy. This last charge seems unfair. *Alroy* is a historical novel, the first Jewish one, but it does not purport to be history, any more than *The Tale of Two Cities* or *Esmond*. Very little has been recorded about the real Alroy, who may have been a self-appointed messiah and whose actual name was

The Dome of the Rock, or Mosque of Omar, in the Muslim (and most salubrious) quarter of Jerusalem. Disraeli made an unsuccessful attempt to enter this mosque, which was strictly forbidden to infidels.

The Pool of Hezekiah, Jerusalem.

The Shrine of the Holy
Sepulchre inside the
Church of that name, the
main focus of Christian
devotion in Jerusalem.
Disraeli noted that this
church 'in its bustle and
lounging character
rather reminded me of an
exchange than a temple'.

Mehemet Ali, ruler of Egypt
1805–1849, with whom
Disraeli had an audience
in Cairo.

A street scene in Cairo in the 1830s, with the Mosque of El Mooristan in the background.

Paul Emile Botta.

The Hon. Edward Stanley,
later 14th Earl of Derby and
three times Prime Minister, as
a young man.

The Great Temple of Abu Simbel, Nubia. Of the ruins in Upper Egypt, Disraeli
wrote: 'My eyes and mind yet ache with grandeur so little in union with our own
littleness.'

Menahem ben Solomon al-Ruhi. He was born in Amadia near the
frontier of Persia. He appears to have led the mountain Jews of
Azerbaijan against their Muslim rulers in the mid-twelfth century,
and, after some success, though nothing like the triumphs described
in *Alroy*, was murdered probably by his father-in-law. Another story
is that, captured by the Caliph, he escaped death with agonizing
torture by declaring that he would miraculously survive, whereupon
the Caliph in a rage ordered his head to be cut off, and so Alroy
expired without pain.

The reality, however, does not matter. What does is the light
thrown by this curious historical romance on Disraeli's mentality
and the effect upon it of his experiences in Syria and Jerusalem. To
get at this the reader has to inure himself to some fairly tedious
passages, for example this excerpt from one of Alroy's soliloquies.

> Hah! what awful form art thou that risest from the dusky
> earth before me? Thou shouldst be one I dare not name, yet
> will: the likeness of Jabaster. Away! why frownest thou upon
> me? I did not slay thee. Do I live, or dream, or what? I see
> him, ay! I see thee. I fear thee not, I fear nothing. I am Alroy.

One feels that Shakespeare had done this sort of thing earlier and
better. Nor does Esther the Prophetess, who plans to murder Alroy
in bed, sound very convincing. She is of course in love with Alroy as
well as dedicated on religious grounds to killing him.

> Can the guilty sleep like the innocent? Who would deem
> this gentle slumberer had betrayed the highest trust that
> ever Heaven vouchsafed to favoured man? He looks not like
> a tyrant and a traitor: calm his brow, and mild his placid
> breath! His long dark hair, dark as the raven's wing, hath
> broken from its fillet and courses, like a wild and stormy
> night, over his pale and moon-lit brow. His cheek is delicate,
> and yet repose hath brought a flush; and on his lip there
> seems some word of love that will not quit it . . . Beauteous
> hero! whether I bear thee most hatred or most love I cannot
> tell. Die thou must, yet I feel I should die with thee. Oh! that

to-night could lead at the same time unto our marriage bed and funeral pyre. Must that white bosom bleed? and must these delicate limbs be hacked and handled by these bloody butchers. . .

Alroy, humiliated at the annual tribute paid by the Jewish community to the Caliph in Bagdad, dreams that he is the Prince of the Captivity destined to lead the Jews to Jerusalem. Jabaster, the archetypal orthodox High Priest, tells him to go first by himself secretly to Jerusalem and obtain the sceptre of Solomon from the Tombs of the Kings. This he duly does, and he raises the standard of revolt in Azerbaijan, defeats the Caliph's forces, enters Bagdad and assumes the Caliphate. In Bagdad he is guided by Honain, Jabaster's brother, the equally archetypal apostate Jew who has been physician to the defeated Caliph and serves whatever regime is in power. Jabaster presses Alroy to march his armies to Jerusalem, but Alroy temporizes. He has fallen in love with Schirene, the daughter of the defeated Caliph, and marries a gentile. The sexual aspect is unequivocal, by the standards of the day. After the lavish grandeur of their wedding celebrations they contemplate next morning's prospect. Should they 'sail upon a cool and azure lake in some bright barque, like to a sea-nymph's shell, and followed by swans? . . . Or shall we launch our falcons in the air, and bring the golden pheasant to our feet?' No, they do neither. 'She threw her arms around his neck and covered his face with kisses.' Their occupation for the day though not described can be surmised. Then, 'Sunset sounded from the minarets. They arose and wandered together in the surrounding paradise.' They are eventually summoned to dinner by 'a dwarf, who, in addition to being very small and very ugly, was dumb,' but he could mime his message. Recumbent on 'a couch covered with a hundred cushions', they are served by a body of slaves 'carrying trays of ivory and gold, ebony and silver, covered with the choicest dainties, curiously prepared'. One of these is 'breast of a cygnet, stuffed with almonds, and stewed with violets and cream'. (Almost any way of making cygnet edible is worth a try, but. . . ?)

Alroy's fortunes now fade. Jabaster is murdered through the machinations of Schirene. Solomon's sceptre abruptly vanishes. Formidable Muslim forces concentrate upon his overthrow. 'The King of Karasme' defeats him in battle. He is later captured and led in bonds to Bagdad sitting on an ass with his back to its head. Honain, always on the winning side, offers him escape from the horrible death of being impaled. He need only bow before 'their Prophet'. Alroy refuses, but escapes torture by taunting the victorious King into cutting off his head at a stroke. 'It fell, and, as it fell, a smile of triumphant derision seemed to play upon the dying features of the hero, and to ask of his enemies, "Where now are your tortures?".' And thus the novel ends – a strange farrago of oriental romance, biblical bombast and dreamy aspiration.

What did Disraeli mean by saying that in *Alroy* he had portrayed his 'ideal ambition'? On the face of things it seems nonsense. Alroy's goal, from which love, reason and indolence diverted him, was to restore Jerusalem to the Jews. It is impossible to envisage Disraeli either doing this or even dreaming that he could. He describes *Alroy* in the preface to his disastrous poem *The Revolutionary Epick* (1834), as 'the celebration of a gorgeous incident in that sacred and romantic people from whom I derive my blood and name'. And this perhaps is the key to his 'ideal ambition'. He saw in the story of David Alroy, embellished and inflated as it is in the novel, the story of an alien who could make his way upwards in a hostile world. The hero of *Contarini Fleming*, though not Jewish, is depicted as engaging in the same sort of struggle. Disraeli clearly identified himself in some degree with both Contarini and Alroy. In their struggles for success he saw mirrored the purpose upon which he was himself already determined. This was to climb to the summit in spite of being an outsider and an adventurer. He also reveals in Alroy's words something of his own doubts, worries, self-pity and *angst*:

I know not what I feel, yet what I feel is madness. Thus to be is not to live, if life be what I sometimes dream and dare to think it might be. To breathe, to feel, to sleep, to wake and breathe again, again to feel existence without hope; if this be life, why then these brooding thoughts that whisper death were better.

Alroy is a strange novel. It is full of absurd extravagancies of the sort already made familiar by Beckford's *Vathek* and similar oriental romances of the day. Beckford, himself a one-time millionaire and the builder of Fonthill, but now retired to Lansdowne Terrace, Bath, was an enthusiast for *Alroy* and, according to Disraeli, wished that 'the truly wondrous tale had been extended to twenty volumes'. The modern reader may feel that the original 'three-decker' was quite long enough. What other novel has eighty-two footnotes to explain the author's part? In the 1878 edition they constitute an appendix of fourteen pages. They are carefully designed to show Disraeli's knowledge, frequently erroneous, of the Alroy legend, the tradition of the Cabala and the practices of the Jewish religion; and they are also a vehicle for describing some of the author's own experiences – for example, Note 7:

> At nightfall, especially in Asia Minor, the lonely horse-man will often meet the jackals on their evening prowl. Their moaning is often heard during the night. I remember, when becalmed off Troy, the most singular screams were heard at intervals throughout the night, from a forest on the opposite shore, which a Greek sailor assured me proceeded from a marten-cat which had probably found the carcase of some horse.

Disraeli believed in making the most of everything that had happened to him. *Alroy* is, though less obviously, almost as autobiographical as *Contarini*. It was a curious book to be published by an author who hoped again to stand for election to Parliament. Whatever else it may have been, it was not exactly a vote-winner among the burgesses of High Wycombe.

3

After *Alroy*, Disraeli seems to have worked Jerusalem, and the East generally, out of his system for the time being. The references to Egypt in *The Vindication* have already been mentioned but otherwise his writings for some years to come show little sign of his oriental experiences. *Henrietta Temple* (December 1836) and *Venetia* (May 1837) deal with other themes. There followed a pause after his marriage and entry into Parliament. But frustrated by failure to secure office from Peel in 1841, he began to take up his pen again. In 1844 he published the first volume of the Trilogy which comprises his three most famous novels: *Coningsby* (1844), which dealt with the condition of political parties, *Sybil* (1845), which discusses 'the condition of the people', and *Tancred* (1847), which is supposed to consider the condition of religion. The Jewish theme is to some extent revived in the first of these by the creation of Sidonia, who utters various observations and apophthegms about Judaism and the Jews, but the scene is more or less confined to England and no one goes to the Holy Land. In *Sybil* there is virtually nothing about the subject.

Tancred, however, is a very different matter. Among the novels of his maturity it is the one that treats Jerusalem and Jewry most seriously and adumbrates most clearly Disraeli's highly eccentric and idiosyncratic views on the relationship between Judaism and Christianity – views which to most Englishmen were either repugnant or incomprehensible. It was surprising that someone seeking a Parliamentary seat in 1833 should have published *Alroy*, but Disraeli was young and relatively obscure. It is unlikely that many of his potential constituents read it or that they made much sense of it if they did. To publish *Tancred* in 1847 was a much riskier step. For a great deal had happened even in the short interval since the appearance of *Sybil*. Disraeli was now a well-known figure and no longer a mere backbencher. He had played a major part in the break-up of the Conservative Party and the fall of Peel in June 1846. He was the principal co-adjutor of Lord George Bentinck who led the Protectionists. When Parliament reassembled in January 1847, he sat with Bentinck on the Opposition front bench. Their followers were the country gentlemen of England, conventional churchmen, agriculturalists and landowners, almost to a man. They had appreciated the wit and satire with which Disraeli had flayed Peel, but they did not greatly trust him, and Lord Stanley, their leader in the House of Lords, who also led the party as a whole, had, as we saw, self-induced reasons for trusting him even less. *Tancred* appearing in March was not calculated to improve this situation. It was bound to attract the maximum of publicity and to be widely reviewed.

Those who attempt to read Disraeli's trilogy usually stop after *Coningsby* and *Sybil*, which are by far the best known of his novels. Only a few go on to *Tancred*, and most of them do not persevere beyond the chapters comprised in Volume I of the original three-volume edition. In a sense they are right. The early chapters, set in the heart of fashionable London society, are much more fun to read than their sequels in Jerusalem. The first volume displays Disraeli in his wittiest and most ironical mood, but it is the second and third in which he is serious, describing the hero's experiences in Syria. They are much less readable than the first, but they have a greater significance in any assessment of his outlook. In 1870 Disraeli wrote a preface to a new collected edition of his novels. He says of *Coningsby*:

> The derivation and character of political parties; the condition of the people which had been the consequence of them; the Church as a main remedial agency in our present state; were the principal topics which I intended to treat, but

I found they were too vast for the space I had allotted to myself.

He goes on to say that he launched these themes in *Coningsby* but could not adequately go beyond the political parties, and that in *Sybil* he considered the condition of the people. Thus he comes to *Tancred*:

> In recognizing the Church as a powerful agent in the previous development of England . . . it seemed to me that the time had arrived when it became my duty . . . to consider the position of the descendants of that race who had been the founders of Christianity. Familiar as we all are now with such themes, the House of Israel being now freed from the barbarism of medieval misconception, and judged like other races by their contribution to the existing sum of human welfare, and the general influence of race on human action being generally recognized as the key to human history, the difficulty and hazard of touching for the first time on such topics cannot now be easily appreciated. But public opinion recognized both the truth and sincerity of these views, and, with its sanction, in TANCRED OR THE NEW CRUSADE, the third portion of the Trilogy, I completed their development.

Disraeli may have recognized the Church 'as a main remedial agency in our present state,' but his picture of the Church of England in *Tancred* is very far from flattering. The story's hero is Tancred, Marquess of Montacute, who has just come of age and is only child and heir to the rich but unworldly Duke of Bellamont. The period seems at first intended to be the Duke of Wellington's premiership of 1828–30, but there are so many anachronistic references that this means little, and we soon move to 1845. Tancred, during his time at Oxford, has been silently brooding on the eternal problems of life and the world since the age of eighteen. He staggers his devoted and solicitous parents by refusing the safe family parliamentary seat vacated for him by a worthy country gentleman, and saying, 'It is the Holy Land that occupies my thought, and I propose to make a pilgrimage to the sepulchre of my Saviour.' This alarming intelligence causes consternation to the Duke. ' "The Holy Land! The Holy Sepulchre!", he exclaimed, and repeated to himself, staring at his son.'

Tancred replies that 'the Creator, since light sprang out of darkness, has deigned to reveal Himself to His creature only in one land; in that land He assumed a manly form and met a human death.' There must be something extraordinary and special about this sacred region. It was the magnet which drew the Crusaders. A De Montacute knelt for three days and three nights 'at the tomb of his Redeemer'; and he goes on:

> It is time to restore and renovate our communications with the Most High. I, too, would kneel at that tomb surrounded by the holy hills and sacred groves of Jerusalem, would relieve my spirit from the bale that bows it down; would lift up my voice to heaven, and ask, What is DUTY, and what is FAITH? What ought I to DO, and what ought I to BELIEVE?

The Duchess is even more alarmed than the Duke:

> 'And it ends in this!' exclaimed the Duchess. 'The Holy Land! Why, if he even reach it, the climate is certain death. The curse of the Almighty for more than eighteen centuries has been on that land. Every year it has become more sterile, more savage, more unwholesome, and more unearthly. It is the abomination of desolation. And now my son is to go there! Oh! he is lost to us for ever!'

How can Tancred be dissuaded from this perilous enterprise? Obviously a cleric is needed, and the Duke and Duchess naturally go to the top. True, most bishops are useless. Disraeli discourses on the appointments of the 'Arch-Mediocrity', i.e. Lord Liverpool, Prime Minister from 1815 to 1827. 'His test of priestly celebrity was the decent editorship of a Greek play. He sought for the successors of the apostles, for the stewards of the mysteries of Sinai and of Calvary, among third-rate hunters after syllables.' In all the convulsions of the time, Disraeli observes:

> Not a voice has been raised by these mitred nullities, either to warn or to vindicate, not a phrase has escaped their lips or their pens, that ever influenced public opinion, touched the heart of nations or guided the conscience of a perplexed people. If they were ever heard of, it was that they had been pelted in a riot.

An exception to this general run of second-rate prelates, though not one whom Disraeli admired, was 'the bishop' – a take-off of Bishop Blomfield (1786–1857), who was Bishop of London from 1828 to his death. He had, in Disraeli's version, a 'ready audacity'. Moreover, 'he combined a great talent for action and very limited powers of thought'.

> Enunciating second-hand, with characteristic precipitation, some big principle in vogue, as if he were a discoverer, he invariably shrank from its subsequent application, the moment that he found it might be unpopular or inconvenient . . . The primordial tenet, which had been advocated with uncompromising arrogance, gently subsided into some second-rate measure recommended with all the artifice of impenetrable ambiguity.

'The bishop' summoned by the Duchess to dissuade Tancred does not get very far. Tancred says that he prefers divine to self-government. 'The bishop' replies that the Church represents God upon earth, to which Tancred answers that the Church no longer governs man.

> 'There is a great spirit rising in the Church,' observed the bishop with thoughtful solemnity; 'a great and excellent spirit. The Church of 1845 is not the Church of 1745. We must remember that; we know not what may happen. We shall soon see a bishop at Manchester.'
> 'But I want to see an angel at Manchester.'

'An angel!'

'Why not? Why should there not be heavenly messengers when heavenly messages are most wanted?'

'We have received a heavenly message by one greater than the angels,' said the bishop, 'their visits to men ceased with the mightier advent.'

'Then why did angels appear to Mary and her companions at the holy tomb?' inquired Tancred.

The bishop fails to answer this conundrum, and 'the interview from which so much was anticipated was not satisfactory.'

Disappointed at spiritual advice, the Duke and Duchess consult their cousin, Lord Eskdale, who is a man of the world. He listens in urbane silence to a long harangue from the Duchess, who declares that she is now convinced that Tancred is 'absolutely more resolved than ever to go to Jerusalem'.

'Well,' said his lordship, 'it is at least better than going to the Jews, which most people do at his time of life.'

'I cannot agree,' said the duchess, 'for I would rather that he should be ruined than die.'

'Men do not die as they used,' said his lordship, 'Ask the annuity offices; they have all raised their rates.'

'I know nothing about annuity offices, but I know that almost everybody dies who goes to those countries. Look at young Fernborough, he was just Tancred's age; the fevers alone must kill him.'

'He must take some quinine in his dressing case,' said Lord Eskdale.

'You jest, Henry,' said the Duchess, 'when I am in despair.'

However, Lord Eskdale has a plan. Pointing out that one cannot go to Jerusalem as to Birmingham, by the next train, he suggests that the Bellamonts can fairly insist that if Tancred makes this visit against their wish, he must at least travel in reasonable safety with a suitable suite on his own yacht. He is sure to have much trouble in buying a second-hand one that pleases him. He will eventually be obliged to have one built. Yacht-building will soon interest him as much as Jerusalem – 'both boyish fancies'. It will take a year. Meanwhile, however shy, he must· move in society. Lord Eskdale will arrange for invitations to 'fall like a snow storm . . . The yacht will be finished this time twelve month; and instead of going to Palestine, he will go to Cowes.'

4

These well-meant efforts at diversion come to nothing. Accompanied by the Montacute factotum, Colonel Brace, and by a chaplain and a doctor, Tancred, equipped with the letter from Sidonia quoted earlier, sets sail for Jerusalem in May 1845. Book III begins in Disraeli's best romantic style:

> The broad moon lingers on the summit of Mount Olivet, but its beam has long left the garden of Gethsemane and the tomb of Absalom, the waters of Kedron and the dark abyss of Jehosaphat. Full falls its splendour, however, on the opposite city, vivid and defined in its silver blaze. A lofty wall, with turrets and towers and frequent gates, undulates with the unequal ground which it covers, as it encircles the lost capital of Jehovah. It is a city of hills far more famous than those of Rome: for all Europe has heard of Sion and Calvary, while the Arab, the Assyrian, and the tribes and nations beyond are as ignorant of the Capitolian and Aventine Mounts as they are of the Malvern or the Chiltern Hills.

Disraeli goes on to describe Jerusalem with a vividness and magniloquence which show that the fifteen years since he sojourned there had not dimmed his memory or blurred his vision. 'Jerusalem by moonlight! 'Tis a fine spectacle apart from all its indissoluble associations of awe and beauty.' No one who has seen it will cavil at those words. He continues:

The moon has sunk behind the Mount of Olives, and the stars in the darker sky shine doubly bright over the sacred city. The all-pervading stillness is broken by a breeze that seems to have travelled over the plain of Sharon from the sea. It wails among the tombs, and sighs among the cypress groves. The palm tree trembles as it passes, as if it were a spirit of woe. Is it the breeze that has travelled over the plain of Sharon from the sea?

Or is it the haunting voice of prophets mourning over the city that they could not save? Their spirits surely would linger on the land where their Creator had deigned to dwell, and over whose impending fate Omnipotence had shed human tears.

Then the camera moves and we see a solitary light in the Church of the Holy Sepulchre. Turkish troops are bivouacked in the forecourt. Two Brothers of the Terra Santa 'keep holy watch and ward; while at the tomb beneath, there kneels a solitary youth, who prostrated himself at sunset, and who will there pass unmoved the whole of the sacred night.' The young man is of course the Marquess of Monta-cute. Tancred has come 'from a distant and a northern isle to bow before the tomb of a descendant of the Kings of Israel, because he, in common with all the people of that isle recognizes in that sublime Hebrew incarnation the presence of a Divine Redeemer'.

The rest of the story, largely an incoherent quasi-mystical oriental farrago of romantic euphoria and dream fulfilment, need not be described here – although it is well worth reading, for in between the nonsense there is some highly entertaining dialogue and many shrewd observations (for example, 'What is the use of belonging to an old family unless to have the authority of an ancestor ready for every prejudice, religious or political, which your combinations [plots] may require?'). Tancred receives no inspiration at Calvary and decides to go to Mt Sinai. He is kidnapped *en route* and he encounters both Eva, who is the incarnation of Judaism, and the Emir Fakredeen, who is the incarnation of oriental intrigue. His captors allow him to go to Sinai where he has a vision of the Angel of Arabia waving 'a sceptre fashioned like a palm tree'. Disraeli finds the ensuing scene unmanageable, and it is one of his least convincing efforts. The Angel tells Tancred:

> Cease, then, to seek in a vain philosophy the solution of the social problem that perplexes you. Announce the sublime and solacing doctrine of theocratic equality. Fear not, faint not, falter not. Obey the impulse of thine own spirit, and find a ready instrument in every human being.

The doctrine of theocratic equality may be sublime and solacing, but it is anything but clear. Unluckily Tancred has no chance to ask, for there is at once a noise of thunder and the vision vanishes, leaving Tancred with an attack of brain fever from which he is only cured by the skill of Eva. Disraeli finds it impossible to bring the plot to a conclusion which makes sense. Tancred declares his love for Eva at dusk in the garden of her house at Bethany. She faints, and he is suddenly interrupted by the sound of many voices. Colonel Brace, the Chaplain, the doctor, his servants enter bearing torches. Tancred asks why he is wanted, and the book ends with that sentence of immortal bathos: 'The Duke and Duchess of Bellamont had arrived in Jerusalem.'

Disraeli regarded *Tancred* as his favourite novel, and, although few people would single it out as his best, one can see why he took that view himself. For in it he expresses some of his deepest feelings – sentiments that had been enhanced and crystallized by his own visit to the Holy Land. Daniel Schwarz[1] shrewdly observes that *Tancred* is quite different from the other novels of the Trilogy, and in a sense ought not to be bracketed with them at all. Neither Coningsby himself, nor Egremont, the hero of *Sybil*, is a romantic figure. Tancred, like his creator, emphatically is. Professor Schwarz describes the book as 'a fictional version of the Victorian spiritual autobiography,' and compares it with others written at about this

[1] *Disraeli's Fiction* (1979), pages 99–100.

time – Anthony Froude's *Shadows of the Clouds*, also published in 1847, Kingsley's *Yeast* and Newman's *Loss and Gain*, both of which appeared a year later. With the exception of *Contarini Fleming*, no other novel by Disraeli is so self-revelatory, so expressive of the author's dreams, fantasies and aspirations. It is, moreover, of all his novels the one that deals most directly with his own ambiguous status in society, a Christianized Jew who wanted to justify both aspects of his life.

The Jews in England were few in number – twenty to thirty thousand in 1815, most of whom lived in London. They were not persecuted but they could be fairly described, in modern jargon, as under-privileged. Neither membership of Parliament nor tenure of the offices of state, administrative and judicial, was open to them, for the oath of loyalty had to be taken 'on the true faith of a Christian'. None of this applied to Isaac D'Israeli's children who had become members of the Church of England in 1817. There was no barrier against people of Jewish descent, only against those of Jewish faith. Indeed some prominent figures of indisputable and unconcealed Jewish origins had made their way in the political world before Disraeli. Sampson Gideon, the younger, the Christianized only son of the great financier, was made a baronet while he was an Eton boy of fifteen, elected to Parliament in 1770 and ended as an Irish peer. David Ricardo, the famous economist, was MP from 1819 to 1823. Ralph Bernal, another Christianized Jew, was actually elected Chairman of Committees in 1830. Sir Manasseh Lopes, having abandoned Judaism in 1802, became a baronet and then entered Parliament. True, he was twice unseated and imprisoned for bribery, but one did not need Jewish ancestry for that achievement.

There was no objection in law to a Christianized Jew holding any position to which he could attain, but there was prejudice in practice. It ranged from the discreet dislike exemplified by Charles Lamb, who did not wish to be 'in habits of familiar intercourse with Jews', to the vulgar abuse of the mob in the Shrewsbury election of 1837 shouting 'Shylock' and 'Old Clothes' at Disraeli for an hour, though they could not stop him being elected. In neither case was much distinction made between a man of Jewish name and one of the Jewish religion. Disraeli was sensitive; the evidence suggests that he was conscious from his adolescence of being different from his school fellows – a youth apart from the rest, and very much aware of the fact. It was natural that someone of his peculiar temperament – ambitious, egotistical, romantic and introspective – should seek some sort of compensatory myth. This was what he found in the east, above all in Jerusalem and Syria.

To console himself for his ambivalent position as a Christianized member of a despised and disliked minority he invented the notion that the Jews were really a superior 'race', and heirs to a civilization, older and greater than that derived from the barbarians who had conquered Europe. In *Contarini Fleming* he writes of his hero:

> Was then this mixed population of Saxons and Normans among whom he had first seen the light, of purer blood than he? Oh no, he was descended in a direct line from one of the oldest races in the world, from that rigidly separate and unmixed Bedouin race who had developed a high civiliza- tion at a time when the inhabitants of England were going half-naked and eating acorns in their woods.

The expression, 'unmixed Bedouin race', is an odd one. What exactly did he mean? The question is not easy to answer, but one can make some headway by remembering that the Arab-versus-Jew syndrome of our time was something that Disraeli would not have understood at all. We are habituated to the antagonism of the Palestinian Arabs, supported by Arab countries all over the east, towards the Israelis, whom they regard as European imperialists, the last bastion of 'colonialism'. But these developments occurred long after the days of Disraeli, who could scarcely be expected to anti- cipate the Balfour Declaration and its consequences. He naturally did not think in those terms at all. To him Jews and Arabs are the same race with different religions. 'The Arabs are only Jews on horseback,' he makes Baroni say in *Tancred* – a sentiment which would not go down well either in modern Jerusalem or modern

Bagdad. What Disraeli seems to be saying is that there is some sort of 'pure Asian breed', as Sidonia puts it, which enjoyed a civilization far older than England. Arabs and Jews are cousins and Disraeli thus stems from an unmixed race of 'Caucasian blood' which is by its very nature aristocratic. There is a passage in *Tancred* which express-es something of all this. Disraeli writes of the Captivity in Egypt that the Jews had become Fellaheen and were made to pay for their sustenance 'as Mehemet Ali has made the Arabs of our day who have quitted the Desert to eat the harvests of the Nile. They enslaved them and worked them as beasts of burden.'

> But this was not to be long borne by a race whose chiefs in the early ages had been favoured by Jehovah; the Patriarch Emirs, who, issuing from the Caucasian cradle of the great races, spread over the plains of Mesopotamia and dissemi-nated their illustrious seed throughout the Arabian wilder-ness. Their fiery imagination brooded over the great tradi-tion of their tribe, and at length there arose among them one of those men whose existence is an epoch in the history of human nature . . .

The man is of course Moses, 'in every respect a man of the complete Caucasian model, and almost as perfect as Adam when he was just finished and placed in Eden'.

> But Jehovah recognized in Moses a human instrument too rare merely to be entrusted with the redemption of an Arabian tribe from a state of Fellaheen to Bedoueen ex-istence. And therefore he was summoned to be the organ of an eternal revelation of the Divine Will, and his tribe were appointed to be the hereditary ministers of that mighty and mysterious dispensation.

The virtues of civilization come from the Near East, but not from its mighty powers.

All the great things have been done by little nations. It is the

Jordan and Ilyssus that have civilized the modern races. An Arabian tribe, a clan of the Aegean, have been the promulgators of all our knowledge; and we should never have heard of the Pharaohs, of Babylon the great and Nineveh the superb, of Cyrus and of Xerxes, had it not been for Athens and Jerusalem.

So Disraeli is heir to a 'race' far older than the forebears of the English nobility. He is not less, indeed he is more aristocratic than a Cavendish. A brilliant chapter in Isaiah Berlin's *Against the Current* is entitled 'Benjamin Disraeli, Karl Marx and the Search for Identity'. The identity which Disraeli sought was found on his tour of the Near East. He was a member of a great race. 'All is race; there is no other truth', as Sidonia says. Disraeli regarded with contempt that 'pernicious doctrine of modern times, the natural equality of man'. He was almost aggressively Jewish and he attributed Jewish ancestry to a number of distinguished people who had nothing of the sort, including Mozart and two of Napoleon's marshals, Soult and Masséna, whose real name he claimed, without the slightest truth, to be Manasseh.

Disraeli came from the fringe of English society. In the book already mentioned, Isaiah Berlin[1] points out how often the most passionate believers in nationalism come from the geographical borders, the remote parts of the country which in some cases they eventually ruled, and with which they identified themselves: Napoleon from Corsica; Stalin from Georgia; Hitler from Austria; De Gaulle from that Lorraine whose cross Winston Churchill found so hard to bear. There are many other examples. Unsure of their position, subject to pressure of alien societies, such figures tend to see their own nation in an over-idealized form. If this can happen with national aspirations, may it not also occur with social aspirations? It is true that Disraeli dwelt geographically in the English heartland, London and Buckinghamshire; but was he really English at all, and where did he stand in terms of English social classification – a young

---

[1] *Against the Current*, pp. 258–9.

middle-class author on the edge of the *beau monde*, a christianized Jew
– 'blank page between the Old Testament and the New'? It is not
surprising that he aspired to enter and rule the aristocratic world,
which at heart he idealized despite his wit and seeming cynicism
about it.

For someone who was content to be a quiet member of a tolerated
minority, like Isaac D'Israeli, no great problem arose. Anti-
semitism was not in those days, nor has it ever been subsequently, a
powerful factor in Britain. Even Mosley himself did not really
believe in it. There has never been much of the dark fanatical lunacy
which from time to time surfaced in Germany and the countries of
Europe further to the east. It is of course true that people have often
made sneering and disagreeable remarks about Jews, and there are
cases even today where people have changed their names from ones
of obvious Jewish origins to something more English-sounding. Yet
in that most significant of all social tests – membership of London
clubs – there has never been a bar to Jews. If Disraeli was black-
balled from the Athenaeum in 1832 it was not because he was a Jew
but because he was regarded – and not without cause – as an insufferable young 'bounder'. He was duly elected thirty-four years later
under the rule which gave, and still gives, priority over ordinary
candidates to a limited number of distinguished persons.

The problem for Disraeli was not anti-semitism but identity. He
was unwilling to be, like his father, a quiet member of a tolerated
minority. He wanted to win, to conquer, to get to the top, to rule. In
order to give himself the driving force, the inner conviction, the
inspiration to do these things he had to create a *persona* and a myth.
This was what his tour of the Near East helped him to do. His
experience may also have coloured his purchase of the Suez Canal
shares, his indifference to the Bulgarian atrocities, his bolstering up
of Turkey, but these are matters of speculation. The important result
was to consolidate his view of his own rôle as a member of a 'race' as
aristocratic, distinguished and great as the English nobility which
controlled English politics and which he aspired not only to join but
to dominate.

5

Disraeli's experience in Jerusalem and its effect on his outlook raises an obvious question. What would he have thought about Israel as a modern state? How would he have viewed the Zionist movement which after so many strange turns and twists of events achieved that seemingly unattainable objective? The orthodox answer is to deny that he thought in those terms at all. 'To suppose that Disraeli was a Zionist is anachronistic and not plausible,' writes Isaiah Berlin. There does, it is true, exist an anonymous pamphlet published in Vienna in 1877 which was attributed to Disraeli by Baron Chlumecki, the Austrian political writer; it favoured the creation of a Jewish state and supported many of the Zionist arguments. There was a good deal of literature on these lines current by then. Chlumecki believed that Disraeli had intended to bring the question up at the Congress of Berlin but was dissuaded by Bismarck, and sent orders to Vienna to suppress the pamphlet of which indeed only one or two copies survive. This inherently unplausible story has been effectively demolished by Cecil Roth[1] and for a multitude of reasons it can be safely dismissed.

There is, however, one episode which has come to light fairly recently and may modify somewhat the usual view of his attitude. The source is the diary of the Lord Stanley who was the son of Disraeli's leader, and later became the 15th Earl of Derby.[2] He has

---

[1] *Benjamin Disraeli* (1952), pp. 159–62.

[2] *Disraeli, Derby and the Conservative Party, the Political Journals of Lord Stanley*, ed. J.R.Vincent (1978).

been described as the type of Plantagenet Palliser in Trollope's political novels. At the time Stanley was a sedate, thoughtful young man of twenty-five who had become a great deal more intimate with Disraeli than was entirely to his father's liking. He spent a week at Hughenden in January 1851 and recorded in 1855 some of his conversations with Disraeli. One that he recalled with particular vividness occurred when they were walking in what was then Lord Carrington's park near Wycombe. It was a very cold day, but Disraeli, though normally sensitive to the temperature, halted so as to emphasize what he was about to say, and appeared impervious to the weather. The subject was the restoration of the Jews to their own land. Disraeli said that the country had excellent natural resources.

> All it wanted was labour and protection for the labourer: the ownership of the soil might be bought from Turkey: money would be forthcoming: the Rothschilds and leading Hebrew capitalists would all help: the Turkish empire was falling into ruin: the Turkish Government would do any-thing for money: all that was necessary was to establish colonies with rights over the soil and security from ill treat-ment. The question of nationality might wait until these had taken hold.

Disraeli went on to say that such ideas were widespread among the Jews and that the man who carried them out 'would be the next Messiah, the true Saviour of his people'. Did he, one wonders, half believe, or dream, that he might like Alroy be that man himself? With Disraeli, it is impossible to tell. He went on to say that there was only one obstacle, 'the existence of two races among the Heb-rews of whom one, those settled along the shores of the Mediterra-nean, look down on the other, refusing even to associate with them. "Sephardism" I think he called the superior race.' Disraeli added that the two great religions of Western Asia and Europe 'were founded by men of Arab blood. It was the race that produced these great results.'

Musing on the matter four years later, Stanley was puzzled, as well he might have been, by this strange conversation. Disraeli seemed to be completely in earnest but he never alluded to the matter in Stanley's presence again. It was the only occasion when 'he ever appeared to me to show signs of any higher emotion'. Was it, Stanley wondered, a 'mystification' (i.e. a hoax)? There was 'certainly nothing in his character to render it unlikely', and Stanley knew of no practical step even suggested by Disraeli during the past four years to achieve his objective. But on the other hand what was the point of a hoax when there was no one else present to enjoy the fun? The puzzle remained a puzzle.

We know today far more about Disraeli in some aspects than Stanley could have known in 1855, though no doubt he had a personal knowledge of others denied to us. One can safely state that, whatever Disraeli was thinking during that frosty winter walk in Lord Carrington's park, he was not trying to hoax or deceive his young friend. What he said was genuine and sincerely meant. Disraeli was fascinated by the thought of the return of the Jews to Palestine. If he took no steps to achieve it, this was mainly because there were none that he could take. It was not a practical proposition in his day or for many years afterwards. It was a dream which became a reality through an extraordinary and wholly unpredictable series of circumstances which neither Disraeli nor anyone else could have foreseen in his lifetime.

The Balfour Declaration split Jewish opinion in Britain in three ways. There were those, like Edwin Montagu, who strongly opposed it as a blow to the long and leisurely process of assimilation which seemed to them to be gaining the day and to be the hope of the future. Others, without such positive hostility to the concept of a national home, were uneasy about its ultimate implications, and wished it had not been made a part of British foreign policy. Yet others greeted it as a great step forward. One cannot doubt where Disraeli would have stood. He surely would have welcomed the Declaration and would have been overjoyed at Allenby's entrance into Jerusalem. He would have remembered his own words about the night breeze on the Mount of Olives – 'the haunting voice of the prophets mourning over a city that they could not save' – and he would have been thrilled at the thought that it might be saved after all.

Index

Aberdeen, Lord, 52
Abu-Ghosh, Sheikhs of, 64, 77
Acre, 63
Adam, General Sir Frederick, 31
Adrianople, Treaty of, 45
Advocate General, at Gibraltar, 14
Albanians, Albania, 29–30, 31, 34,
    34–5, 38, 39, 83, 110
Alexander, Michael Solomon, 78
Alexandria, 81
Algiers, 18
Alhambra, 16, 17
Ali Pasha, 51
Alroy, David, 110–11
Amin Pacha, 39–40
anti-semitism, 129
Arimathea, see Ramle
Armenians, Armenia, 55, 75, 76–7
Arta, 34
Assyria, 98
Athenaeum club, 129
Athens, 31, 45, 47–8, 65–6
Austen, Benjamin, 5, 6, 8, 18
Austen, Sara, 5, 8

Balfour Declaration, 132
Balmoral, 53
Beckford, William, 114

Bentham, Jeremy, 32
Bentinck, Lord George, 116
Berlin, Congress of, 31, 130
Berlin, Sir Isaiah, 128, 130
Bernal, Ralph, 125
Bithynian mountains, 53
Blomfield, Bishop, 119
Bolton, Dr Buckley, 5
Bolton, Clara, 5–6
Bond, Effie, 100–1
Bosphorus, 54–5
Botta, Paul Emile, 97–100
Bradenham, 5, 37, 56, 88
Britain
    and Ionian Islands, 29
    politics in, 18, 53–4, 85–6, 116
    and Turkey, 30, 51–2, 73, 78
Broadfoot, Dr Alexander, 11
Brougham, Henry, 54
Brunet (manservant), 13–14
Bulgarian atrocities, 58
Bulwer-Lytton, Henry, 7
Bulwer-Lytton, Edward (later
    Lord Lytton), 7, 8, 47, 97, 110
Byron, Lord, 8, 19, 30, 33

Cadiz, 14
Cairo, 90, 92–3, 96, 97

Capodistria, Count Ioannes
    Antonios, 45
Chalcedon, Council of, 75
Chlumecki, Baron, 130
Choiseul, Duc de, 82
Christians, and Jerusalem, 72–8
    passim, 107
Clarke, Rev. E. D., 67–8
Clay, James, 19–22
    joins Tour with yacht, 19, 24–5
    his sexual prowess, 19–21
    D'Israeli family's disapproval of,
        21
    Disraeli's relations with, 21–2,25
    mentioned during Tour, 23, 24,
        31, 35, 36, 48, 62, 78, 81, 85,97
    on Disraeli's need of a nurse, 87
    his illness in Egypt, 87, 92, 93,105
    leaves Cairo to organize return
        voyage, 99
    returns via Malta, 20, 100
Clay, Sir William, 19
Cockburn, Alexander, 7
Codrington, Admiral, 45
Colburn, Henry, 4, 6, 109
Constantinople, 49, 50, 52, 54–5,
    56–7
Cordova, 16
Corfu, 29
Corinth, 46–7
Corney, Bolton, 9
Cyclades, 6, 46, 49
Cyprus, 62–3

Damiani, 63
Dardanelles, 49
Dendera, 91, 92

Derby, Earls of, *see* Stanley
desert, Egyptian, 91
D'Israeli, Benjamin (father of
    Isaac), 8–9
Disraeli, Benjamin
    amorous affairs, 5–6, 20, 25, 93, 98
    baptised into Church of
        England, 74
    business speculations, debts,
        3–4, 6
    conspiracy, intrigue, attitude to,
        56
    dress, foppish behaviour, wit,6–7,
        14, 22–3, 25, 47
    education, 10
    Englishness, doubts as to his,
        128–9
    family, relations with (see also
        Home Letters, below), 8–10, 88–9
    food, comments on, 13, 15, 34,
        36, 63, 81, 89
    Grand Tour, preparations for,6–7
    Grand Tour, progress of, *see*
        Falmouth; Gibraltar; Spain;
        Malta; Greece; Constanti-
        nople; Smyrna; Cyprus; Jaffa;
        Jerusalem; Egypt
    Grand Tour, effects of, 3, 105–33
    health, 3, 5, 15, 15–16, 17, 31, 53,
        57, 62, 87, 88, 102, 105–6
    and Jews, Jewishness, 9, 74,
        75–7, 106–8, 110–14, 115–33
    men, conversation with, his
        views on, 97
    and Moslem culture (*see also*
        Turkey, *below*), 16, 31, 34, 57,
        93

nurse, his need of, alleged, 87

political attitudes and opinions
(*see also* Jews, *above*), 3, 30,
52, 54, 56, 57–8, 85–6, 93–6,
113, 115, 116–17

servants, comments on, 13–14,
19, 87–8

smoking, 24, 47, 88, 89

Switzerland and Italy, visit to
(1826), 5

travel, comments on, 7–8, 17–18,
29, 46, 48–9, 62, 64

Turkey and Greece, his views on,
29–31, 32, 47, 50, 52

Alroy, see *Wondrous Tale of Alroy*,
below

Coningsby, 115, 116–17, 124

Contarini Fleming, 3, 15, 40–1, 61,
65, 69, 70–1, 109, 113, 126

Henrietta Temple, 115

Home Letters (number of, dates,
etc.; quotations from the Letters
appear throughout and are not
indexed), 8, 11, 15, 16, 22, 34,
40, 53, 57, 69, 85, 106, 109

Lothair, 3

'Mutilated Diary', 97

novels, influenced by Grand
Tour, 3, 109–14, 115–24

pamphlets for Murray (1825), 4

publishers, *see* Colburn; Murray;
Saunders and Otley

Revolutionary Epick, The, 113

Rise of Iskander, The, 109, 110

Sybil, 115, 117, 124

Tancred, 3, 75–7, 78, 107–8, 109,
115–25, 126–8

Venetia, 30, 115

*Vindication of the English Constitu-
tion*, 93–6

Vivian Grey, 3, 4–5, 12, 109

Voyage of Captain Popanilla, The, 5

Wondrous Tale of Alroy, The, 3, 6,
61, 70, 109, 110, 110–14, 115–16

Young Duke, The, 6

D'Israeli, Coningsby (son of
Ralph), 10

D'Israeli, Isaac (father of
Benjamin Disraeli), 3, 5, 6,
7, 8–9,74, 88, 89, 129

D'Israeli, James (brother of
Benjamin), 10, 88–9

D'Israeli, Maria (mother of
Benjamin), 8, 9

D'Israeli, Ralph (brother of
Benjamin), 8, 10, 19, 85, 89

D'Israeli, Sarah (sister of
Benjamin), 6, 7, 8, 10, 21, 22,
88, 100

D'Israeli family, origins of, 9

Don, Sir George, 11–12

Eastern Question, 3; *see also* Berlin,
Congress of; Bulgarian
atrocities; Turks

Ecarté (card game), 22

Egypt
Disraeli and, 62, 81, 85, 90–6, 97,
99–100
history of, 66, 82–4; *see also*
Mehemet Ali; *and under* Turks

Epirus, 34

Falcieri, Giovanni Battista ('Tita'),
    19, 21, 35, 36, 87
Falmouth, 7–8
Ferdinand vii, King, of Spain, 12
Filioque, 75
Fortunatus, 62–3
France, 52, 73, 75, 82–3
Franciscan Order, 67
Franz-Joseph, Emperor, 65
Froude, Anthony, 125

Galignani's Messenger, 53, 85
Gibbon, Edward, 110
Gibraltar, 8, 11–12, 14, 16, 17
Gideon, Sampson, 125
Gladstone, William Ewart, 29, 30,
    47
Glentworth, Lord, *see* Pery,
    Edmund
Gordon, Sir Robert, 52–3, 61
Granada, 15, 16
Greece
    Disraeli and, 29–41, 45–9, 65–6
    history of, 29–33, 34, 39, 45, 47
Grey, Earl, 54

Habsburg Empire, 52
Hamilton, W. R., 62
High Wycombe, by-election at
    (1832), 30, 114
Holy Sepulchre, Church of the,
    Jerusalem, 69, 75, 123
Hughenden Manor, 10, 19
Hughes, Thomas, 32
Hutchinson, General, 83

Ibrahim (son of Mehemet Ali), 33,
    45, 77, 78
Ionian Islands, 29, 46
Islam, 50, 72, 107
    Disraeli and, *see* Moslem culture
        under Disraeli
    see also Turks

Jaffa, 63–4, 83
Janissaries, 51
Jerusalem, 63–78
    Christians in, 72–8 *passim*
    Disraeli impressed by, 65–6, 69,
        106
    Disraeli's journey to, 63–5
    Disraeli's reasons for visiting, 61
    Dome of the Rock (Mosque of
        Omar), 66, 70, 72
    Holy Sepulchre, Church of the,
        69, 75, 123
    Jews in, 72–8 *passim*
    political and social condition of,
        70–8
    St Salvador, monastery of, 66–8
    in *Tancred*, 75–6, 107–8, 122–3
    view of, from Mount of Olives,
        65–6
    wall of, 65, 66
    in *The Wondrous Tale of Alroy*, 112
    see also Zionism
Jews
    in Constantinople, 55
    Disraeli and, *see under* Disraeli
    in England, 125, 129
    in 'Syria', Jerusalem, 72–8 *passim*
    see also Jerusalem; Zionism

Kalio Bey, 34–5
Kingsley, Charles, 125

Lamb, Charles, 125
Layard, Sir Henry, 98, 99
Leibniz, Gottfried Wilhelm, 82
Leopold of Coburg, 45
Liddell, George, 24
Liverpool, Lord, 118
Lockhart, J. G., 4
London, Treaty of (1827), 33
London Jewish Society, 78
Lopes, Sir Manasseh, 125
Lords, House of, 94
Louis, King, of Bavaria, 45
Louis XIV, King, of France, 82
Lyndhurst, Lord, 93

Mahmoud II, Sultan, 32, 33, 51, 52, 55–6
malaria, 105
Malta, 17–18, 20, 22–5, 100
Mamelukes, 51, 82–3, 84
Martin, John, 66, 92
Max (Newfoundland puppy), 89–90
Mehemet Ali, Pasha of Egypt, 33, 51, 77, 81, 83–4, 93–6
Meredith, William, 6, 7–8
    comments on Disraeli, 6–7, 16, 25*n.*
    mentioned during Tour, 11, 12, 13, 14, 16, 17, 22, 31, 36, 48
    and Clay, 19, 22, 24–5
    leaves party to explore Bithynian

    mountains, 53
    rejoins party at Smyrna, but leaves again, 62
    and Egypt, 62, 81, 86, 91, 97, 99
    Disraeli's account of their parting, 86
    his death, 99–100
Meyer, Mr, 34
Moldavia and Wallachia, 45
Monophysites, 75
Montagu, Edwin, 132
Montefiore, Sir Moses, 66, 74
Moses, 127
Moslem culture, *see* Islam
Mosely, Sir Oswald, 129
muezzin, 34
Murray, John 4–5, 9, 109

Nairoli, 88
Napoleon Bonaparte, 23, 82–3
nationalism, 30, 32–3, 128; *see also* Zionism
Nauplion, 46
Navarino, 33, 46
Near East, unhealthy, 105
Nelson, Lord, 83
Newman, John Henry, Cardinal, 125
Nile, river, 90, 90–2
Nile, Battle of the, 83
Normanby, Lady, 22

olio (Spanish dish), 15
Olives, Mount of, 65–6

Omar, Mosque of, *see* Rock, Dome of the
Otto, Prince, of Bavaria, 45
Ottoman Empire, *see* Turks
Oxford University, 9

Palestine, 63, 72; *see also* Jerusalem; Syria
Palmerston, Lord, 29, 53
parliamentary reform, 54, 85–6
Peel, Sir Robert, 115, 116
Pery, Edmund (later Lord Glentworth), 24
politics, *see* Eastern Question; *see also under* Britain *and* Disraeli
Ponsonby, Sir Frederick, 23
Powles, J. D., 4
Prevesa, 32, 34, 40
Prussia, and Jerusalem Protestants, 73, 78
Pyramids, 90

Ramle (Arimathea), 64
Reform Bill, *see* parliamentary reform
Representative, 4
Reschid Mehmet Pasha, 31, 38–40
Rhodes, 62
Ricardo, David, 125
Rock, Dome of the (Mosque of Omar), 66, 70, 72
Rose, Sir Philip, 21, 100–1
Rosetta, 90
Rosetta Stone, 62
Roth, Cecil, 130

Russia, and Turkey, 30, 45, 51–2, 56, 73, 75

Safed, 72
St Nicodemus and St Joseph of Arimathea, Hospice of, 64
St Salvador, monastery of, 66–8
Saunders and Otley, 109
Schwarz, Daniel, 124–5
Scott, Sir Walter, 8
Selim I, Sultan, 66, 82
Seville, 14–15, 16, 17
Seymour, George, 52
Shelley, Percy Bysshe, 19
Shrewsbury, election at (1837), 125
Sierra da Ronda, 12
Simoom, 91
Skanderbeg, 110
smallpox, 99–100, 105
Smith, Sir Sidney, 83
Smyrna, 62
Southey, Robert, 8
Spain, 12–14, 14–17
Spencer, Rev. J. A., 71, 73–4
Stanley, Edward Geoffrey Smith, Lord (later 14th Earl of Derby), 100, 101, 116
Stanley, Edward Henry Smith, Lord (later 15th Earl of Derby), 47, 130–2
Stanley, Henry, 100–1
Suleiman the Magnificent, Sultan, 66
Sunium, 49
Sykes, Henrietta, 24, 93
Syria, 63, 66, 77; *see also* Jerusalem

Taunton, by-election at (1835), 30
Thebes, 91, 92
'Tita', *see* Falcieri, Giovanni
    Battista
tomato sauce, 15
Turks, Turkey, Ottoman Empire,
    50–2, 107
  Armenian massacre, 77
  Disraeli and, *see under* Disraeli
  and Egypt, 66, 77–8, 82–4
  and Greece, Albania, 29–33, 34,
    35–41, 45, 47
  and Syria, Jerusalem, 66, 70, 73,
    75, 77–8
  see also Constantinople;
    Mahmoud II

Ulema, 84

Venice, 20–1, 29
Villebois, Eve, 24
Villiers, Charles, 7

Wellington, Duke of, 30, 53–4
Wilkinson, Sir John, 92
William IV, King, 18, 85

Yanina, 31, 37–40

Zante, 46
Zea, 61
Zionism, 130–3